Cambridge IELTS 5

Examination papers from University of Cambridge ESOL Examinations: English for Speakers of Other Languages

CAMBRIDGE
UNIVERSITY PRESS

CAMBRIDGE UNIVERSITY PRESS
Cambridge, New York, Melbourne, Madrid, Cape Town, Singapore, São Paulo, Delhi

Cambridge University Press
10 Hoe Chiang Road, #08-01/02 Keppel Towers, Singapore 089315.

www.cambridge.org
Information on this title: www.cambridge.org/9780521698894

First published 2006
This China edition first published 2006
Sixth printing 2008

Printed in Singapore by Craftprint International Ltd

A catalogue record for this book is available from the British Library

ISBN-13   978-0-521-67701-1 Student's Book with answers

ISBN-13   978-0-521-67703-5 Cassette Set

ISBN-13   978-0-521-67704-2 Audio CD Set

ISBN-13   978-0-521-67702-8 Self-study Pack

ISBN-13   978-0-521-69889-4 Self-study Pack China Edition

This special edition is for sale in mainland China only.
It is not for sale in Hong Kong SAR, Macau SAR and Taiwan Province.

Contents

Introduction

The International English Language Testing System (IELTS) is widely recognised as a reliable means of assessing the language ability of candidates who need to study or work where English is the language of communication. These Practice Tests are designed to give future IELTS candidates an idea of whether their English is at the required level.

IELTS is owned by three partners: the University of Cambridge ESOL Examinations, the British Council and IDP: Education Australia (through its subsidiary company, IELTS Australia Pty Limited).

Further information on IELTS can be found in the IELTS Handbook and the IELTS Information for candidates leaflet, available free of charge from IELTS centres. These can also be downloaded from the IELTS website (www.ielts.org).

WHAT IS THE TEST FORMAT?

IELTS consists of six modules. All candidates take the same Listening and Speaking modules. There is a choice of Reading and Writing modules according to whether a candidate is taking the Academic or General Training version of the test.

Academic	General Training
For candidates taking the test for entry to undergraduate or postgraduate studies or for professional reasons.	For candidates taking the test for entry to vocational or training programmes not at degree level, for admission to secondary schools and for immigration purposes.

The test modules are taken in the following order:

Listening
4 sections, 40 items
approximately 30 minutes

Academic Reading		General Training Reading
3 sections, 40 items	OR	3 sections, 40 items
60 minutes		60 minutes

Academic Writing		General Training Writing
2 tasks	OR	2 tasks
60 minutes		60 minutes

Speaking
11 to 14 minutes

Total Test Time
2 hours 44 minutes

Listening

This module consists of four sections, each with ten questions. The first two sections are concerned with social needs. The first section is a conversation between two speakers and the second section is a monologue. The final two sections are concerned with situations related to educational or training contexts. The third section is a conversation between up to four people and the fourth section a monologue.

A variety of question types is used, including: multiple choice, short-answer questions, sentence completion, notes/form/table/summary/flow-chart completion, labelling a diagram/plan/map, classification, matching.

Candidates hear the recording once only and answer the questions as they listen. Ten minutes are allowed at the end for candidates to transfer their answers to the answer sheet.

Academic Reading

This module consists of three sections with 40 questions. There are three reading passages, which are taken from magazines, journals, books and newspapers. The passages are on topics of general interest. At least one passage contains detailed logical argument.

A variety of question types is used, including: multiple choice, short-answer questions, sentence completion, notes/summary/flow-chart/table completion, labelling a diagram, classification, matching, choosing suitable paragraph headings from a list, identification of writer's views/claims – *yes, no, not given* – or identification of information in the passage – *true, false, not given.*

General Training Reading

This module consists of three sections with 40 questions. The texts are taken from notices, advertisements, leaflets, newspapers, instruction manuals, books and magazines. The first section contains texts relevant to basic linguistic survival in English, with tasks mainly concerned with providing factual information. The second section focuses on the training context and involves texts of more complex language. The third section involves reading more extended texts, with a more complex structure, but with the emphasis on descriptive and instructive rather than argumentative texts.

A variety of question types is used, including: multiple choice, short-answer questions, sentence completion, notes/summary/flow-chart/table completion, labelling a diagram, classification, matching, choosing suitable paragraph headings from a list, identification of writer's views/claims – *yes, no, not given* – identification of information in the text – *true, false, not given.*

Academic Writing

This module consists of two tasks. It is suggested that candidates spend about 20 minutes on Task 1, which requires them to write at least 150 words, and 40 minutes on Task 2, which requires them to write at least 250 words. The assessment of Task 2 carries more weight in marking than Task 1.

Task 1 requires candidates to look at a diagram or some data (graph, table or chart) and to present the information in their own words. They are assessed on their ability to organise, present and possibly compare data, describe the stages of a process, describe an object or event, or explain how something works.

In Task 2 candidates are presented with a point of view, argument or problem. They are assessed on their ability to present a solution to the problem, present and justify an opinion, compare and contrast evidence and opinions, and evaluate and challenge ideas, evidence or arguments.

Candidates are also assessed on their ability to write in an appropriate style.

General Training Writing

This module consists of two tasks. It is suggested that candidates spend about 20 minutes on Task 1, which requires them to write at least 150 words, and 40 minutes on Task 2, which requires them to write at least 250 words. The assessment of Task 2 carries more weight in marking than Task 1.

In Task 1 candidates are asked to respond to a given problem with a letter requesting information or explaining a situation. They are assessed on their ability to engage in personal correspondence, elicit and provide general factual information, express needs, wants, likes and dislikes, express opinions, complaints, etc.

In Task 2 candidates are presented with a point of view, argument or problem. They are assessed on their ability to provide general factual information, outline a problem and present a solution, present and justify an opinion, and evaluate and challenge ideas, evidence or arguments.

Candidates are also judged on their ability to write in an appropriate style.

Speaking

This module takes between 11 and 14 minutes and is conducted by a trained examiner.

There are three parts:

Part 1
The candidate and the examiner introduce themselves. Candidates then answer general questions about themselves, their home/family, their job/studies, their interests and a wide range of similar familiar topic areas. This part lasts between four and five minutes.

Part 2
The candidate is given a task card with prompts and is asked to talk on a particular topic. The candidate has one minute to prepare and they can make some notes if they wish, before speaking for between one and two minutes. The examiner then asks one or two rounding-off questions.

Part 3
The examiner and the candidate engage in a discussion of more abstract issues which are thematically linked to the topic prompt in Part 2. The discussion lasts between four and five minutes.

The Speaking module assesses whether candidates can communicate effectively in English. The assessment takes into account Fluency and Coherence, Lexical Resource, Grammatical Range and Accuracy, and Pronunciation.

HOW IS IELTS SCORED?

IELTS results are reported on a nine-band scale. In addition to the score for overall language ability, IELTS provides a score in the form of a profile for each of the four skills (Listening, Reading, Writing and Speaking). These scores are also reported on a nine-band scale. All scores are recorded on the Test Report Form along with details of the candidate's nationality, first language and date of birth. Each Overall Band Score corresponds to a descriptive statement which gives a summary of the English language ability of a candidate classified at that level. The nine bands and their descriptive statements are as follows:

9 Expert User – *Has fully operational command of the language: appropriate, accurate and fluent with complete understanding.*

8 Very Good User – *Has fully operational command of the language with only occasional unsystematic inaccuracies and inappropriacies. Misunderstandings may occur in unfamiliar situations. Handles complex detailed argumentation well.*

7 Good User – *Has operational command of the language, though with occasional inaccuracies, inappropriacies and misunderstandings in some situations. Generally handles complex language well and understands detailed reasoning.*

6 Competent User – *Has generally effective command of the language despite some inaccuracies, inappropriacies and misunderstandings. Can use and understand fairly complex language, particularly in familiar situations.*

5 Modest User – *Has partial command of the language, coping with overall meaning in most situations, though is likely to make many mistakes. Should be able to handle basic communication in own field.*

4 Limited User – *Basic competence is limited to familiar situations. Has frequent problems in understanding and expression. Is not able to use complex language.*

3 Extremely Limited User – *Conveys and understands only general meaning in very familiar situations. Frequent breakdowns in communication occur.*

2 Intermittent User – *No real communication is possible except for the most basic information using isolated words or short formulae in familiar situations and to meet immediate needs. Has great difficulty understanding spoken and written English.*

1 Non User – *Essentially has no ability to use the language beyond possibly a few isolated words.*

0 Did not attempt the test. – *No assessable information provided.*

Most universities and colleges in the United Kingdom, Australia, New Zealand and Canada accept an IELTS Overall Band Score of 6.0 or 6.5 for entry to academic programmes. IELTS scores are recognised by over 500 universities and colleges in the USA.

MARKING THE PRACTICE TESTS

Listening and Reading

The Answer key is on pages 152–161.
Each question in the Listening and Reading modules is worth one mark.

Questions which require letter/Roman numeral answers
- For questions where the answers are letters or numbers, you should write *only* the number of answers required. For example, if the answer is a single letter or number you should write only one answer. If you have written more letters or numerals than are required, the answer must be marked wrong.

Questions which require answers in the form of words or numbers
- Answers may be written in upper or lower case.
- Words in brackets are *optional* – they are correct, but not necessary.
- Alternative answers are separated by a single slash (/).
- If you are asked to write an answer using a certain number of words and/or (a) number(s), you will be penalised if you exceed this. For example if a question specifies an answer using NO MORE THAN THREE WORDS and the correct answer is 'black leather coat', the answer of 'coat of black leather' is *incorrect*.
- In questions where you are expected to complete a gap, you should transfer only the necessary missing word(s) onto the answer sheet. For example, to complete 'in the . . .', and the correct answer is 'morning', the answer 'in the morning' would be *incorrect*.
- All answers require correct spelling (including words in brackets).
- Both US and UK spelling are acceptable and are included in the Answer key.
- All standard alternatives for numbers, dates and currencies are acceptable.
- All standard abbreviations are acceptable.
- You will find additional notes about individual questions in the Answer key.

Writing

It is not possible for you to give yourself a mark for the Writing tasks. For *Task 1* in *Tests 1 and 3*, and *Task 2* in *Tests 2 and 4*, and for *Task 1* in *General Training Test A* and *Task 2* in *General Training Test B*, we have provided *model answers* (written by an examiner) at the back of the book. It is important to note that these show just one way of completing the task, out of many possible approaches. For *Task 2* in *Tests 1 and 3*, *Task 1* in *Tests 2 and 4*, *Task 2* in *General Training Test A* and *Task 1* in *General Training Test B*, we have provided *sample answers* (written by candidates), showing their score and the examiner's comments. These model answers and sample answers will give you an insight into what is required for the Writing module.

HOW SHOULD YOU INTERPRET YOUR SCORES?

In the Answer key at the end of each set of Listening and Reading answers you will find a chart which will help you assess whether, on the basis of your Practice Test results, you are ready to take the IELTS test.

In interpreting your score, there are a number of points you should bear in mind. Your performance in the real IELTS test will be reported in two ways: there will be a Band Score from 1 to 9 for each of the modules and an Overall Band Score from 1 to 9, which is the average of your scores in the four modules. However, institutions considering your application are advised to look at both the Overall Band and the Bands for each module in order to determine whether you have the language skills needed for a particular course of study. For example, if your course has a lot of reading and writing, but no lectures, listening skills might be less important and a score of 5 in Listening might be acceptable if the Overall Band Score was 7. However, for a course which has lots of lectures and spoken instructions, a score of 5 in Listening might be unacceptable even though the Overall Band Score was 7.

Once you have marked your tests you should have some idea of whether your listening and reading skills are good enough for you to try the IELTS test. If you did well enough in one module but not in others, you will have to decide for yourself whether you are ready to take the test.

The Practice Tests have been checked to ensure that they are of approximately the same level of difficulty as the real IELTS test. However, we cannot guarantee that your score in the Practice Tests will be reflected in the real IELTS test. The Practice Tests can only give you an idea of your possible future performance and it is ultimately up to you to make decisions based on your score.

Different institutions accept different IELTS scores for different types of courses. We have based our recommendations on the average scores which the majority of institutions accept. The institution to which you are applying may, of course, require a higher or lower score than most other institutions.

Sample answers and model answers are provided for the Writing tasks. The sample answers were written by IELTS candidates; each answer has been given a band score and the candidate's performance is described. Please note that there are many different ways by which a candidate may achieve a particular band score. The model answers were written by an examiner as examples of very good answers, but it is important to understand that they are just one example out of many possible approaches.

Further information

For more information about IELTS or any other University of Cambridge ESOL examination write to:

University of Cambridge ESOL Examinations
1 Hills Road
Cambridge
CB1 2EU
United Kingdom

Telephone: +44 1223 553355
Fax: +44 1223 460278
e-mail: ESOLhelpdesk@cambridgeassessment.org.uk
http://www.cambridgeesol.org
http://www.ielts.org

Test 1

SECTION 1   *Questions 1–10*

Questions 1–6

Complete the notes below.

*Write **NO MORE THAN TWO WORDS AND/OR A NUMBER** for each answer.*

Dreamtime travel agency
Tour information

Example	Answer
Holiday name	<u>Whale Watch</u> Experience

Holiday length	2 days
Type of transportation	**1** ....
Maximum group size	**2** ....
Next tour date	**3** ....
Hotel name	**4** The ....

Questions 5 and 6

*Choose **TWO** letters A–E.*

*Which **TWO** things are included in the price of the tour?*

    A   fishing trip
    B   guided bushwalk
    C   reptile park entry
    D   table tennis
    E   tennis

Questions 7–10

Complete the sentences below.

*Write **NO MORE THAN THREE WORDS AND/OR A NUMBER** for each answer.*

7   The tour costs $......................... .

8   Bookings must be made no later than .... days in advance.

9   A .... deposit is required.

10   The customer's reference number is ....

SECTION 2   *Questions 11–20*

Questions 11–19

Complete the table below.

*Write **NO MORE THAN THREE WORDS** for each answer.*

Brand of Cot	Good Points	Problems	Verdict
Baby Safe	Easy to 11	• Did not have any 12 .... • Babies could trap their 13 .... in the side bar	14 ....
Choice Cots	Easy to 15	• Side did not drop down • Spaces between the bars were 16	17 ....
Mother's Choice	Base of cot could be moved	• Did not have any 18 .... • Pictures could be removed easily	19 ....

Question 20

Complete the notes below.

*Write **ONE WORD ONLY** for the answer.*

- Metal should not be rusted or bent
- Edges of cot should not be **20** ....

SECTION 3   *Questions 21–30*

Questions 21–23

*Choose the correct letter, **A**, **B** or **C**.*

21   Andrew has worked at the hospital for

   A   two years.
   B   three years.
   C   five years.

22   During the course Andrew's employers will pay

   A   his fees.
   B   his living costs.
   C   his salary.

23   The part-time course lasts for

   A   one whole year.
   B   18 months.
   C   two years.

Questions 24 and 25

*Choose **TWO** letters A–E.*

*What **TWO** types of coursework are required **each month** on the part-time course?*

   A   a case study
   B   an essay
   C   a survey
   D   a short report
   E   a study diary

Questions 26–30

Complete the summary below.

Write **NO MORE THAN THREE WORDS AND/OR A NUMBER** *for each answer.*

Modular Courses

Students study **26** .... during each module. A module takes
27 .... and the work is very **28** .... To get a Diploma each
student has to study **29** .... and then work on **30** ....
in depth.

SECTION 4   *Questions 31–40*

Questions 31–35

Complete the sentences below.

*Write **NO MORE THAN THREE WORDS** for each answer.*

31   According to George Bernard Shaw, men are supposed to understand .... , economics and finance.

32   However, women are more prepared to .... about them.

33   Women tend to save for .... and a house.

34   Men tend to save for .... and for retirement.

35   Women who are left alone may have to pay for .... when they are old.

Questions 36–40

Complete the summary below.

*Write **NO MORE THAN THREE WORDS AND/OR A NUMBER** for each answer.*

Saving for the future

Research indicates that many women only think about their financial future when a **36** .... occurs. This is the worst time to make decisions. It is best for women to start thinking about pensions when they are in their **37** .... A good way for women to develop their **38** .... in dealing with financial affairs would be to attend classes in **39** .... When investing in stocks and shares, it is suggested that women should put a high proportion of their savings in **40** .... In such ways, women can have a comfortable, independent retirement.

READING

READING PASSAGE 1

*You should spend about 20 minutes on **Questions 1–13**, which are based on Reading Passage 1 below.*

Johnson's Dictionary

For the century before Johnson's *Dictionary* was published in 1775, there had been concern about the state of the English language. There was no standard way of speaking or writing and no agreement as to the best way of bringing some order to the chaos of English spelling. Dr Johnson provided the solution.

There had, of course, been dictionaries in the past, the first of these being a little book of some 120 pages, compiled by a certain Robert Cawdray, published in 1604 under the title *A Table Alphabeticall* 'of hard usuall English wordes'. Like the various dictionaries that came after it during the seventeenth century, Cawdray's tended to concentrate on 'scholarly' words; one function of the dictionary was to enable its student to convey an impression of fine learning.

Beyond the practical need to make order out of chaos, the rise of dictionaries is associated with the rise of the English middle class, who were anxious to define and circumscribe the various worlds to conquer – lexical as well as social and commercial. It is highly appropriate that Dr Samuel Johnson, the very model of an eighteenth-century literary man, as famous in his own time as in ours, should have published his *Dictionary* at the very beginning of the heyday of the middle class.

Johnson was a poet and critic who raised common sense to the heights of genius. His approach to the problems that had worried writers throughout the late seventeenth and early eighteenth centuries was intensely practical. Up until his time, the task of producing a dictionary on such a large scale had seemed impossible without the establishment of an academy to make decisions about right and wrong usage. Johnson decided he did not need an academy to settle arguments about language; he would write a dictionary himself; and he would do it single-handed. Johnson signed the contract for the *Dictionary* with the bookseller Robert Dosley at a breakfast held at the Golden Anchor Inn near Holborn Bar on 18 June 1764. He was to be paid £1,575 in instalments, and from this he took money to rent 17 Gough Square, in which he set up his 'dictionary workshop'.

James Boswell, his biographer, described the garret where Johnson worked as 'fitted up like a counting house' with a long desk running down the middle at which the copying clerks would work standing up.

Johnson himself was stationed on a rickety chair at an 'old crazy deal table' surrounded by a chaos of borrowed books. He was also helped by six assistants, two of whom died whilst the *Dictionary* was still in preparation.

The work was immense; filling about eighty large notebooks (and without a library to hand), Johnson wrote the definitions of over 40,000 words, and illustrated their many meanings with some 114,000 quotations drawn from English writing on every subject, from the Elizabethans to his own time. He did not expect to achieve complete originality. Working to a deadline, he had to draw on the best of all previous dictionaries, and to make his work one of heroic synthesis. In fact, it was very much more. Unlike his predecessors, Johnson treated English very practically, as a living language, with many different shades of meaning. He adopted his definitions on the principle of English common law – according to precedent. After its publication, his *Dictionary* was not seriously rivalled for over a century.

After many vicissitudes the *Dictionary* was finally published on 15 April 1775. It was instantly recognised as a landmark throughout Europe. 'This very noble work,' wrote the leading Italian lexicographer, 'will be a perpetual monument of Fame to the Author, an Honour to his own Country in particular, and a general Benefit to the republic of Letters throughout Europe.' The fact that Johnson had taken on the Academies of Europe and matched them (everyone knew that forty French academics had taken forty years to produce the first French national dictionary) was cause for much English celebration.

Johnson had worked for nine years, 'with little assistance of the learned, and without any patronage of the great; not in the soft obscurities of retirement, or under the shelter of academic bowers, but amidst inconvenience and distraction, in sickness and in sorrow'. For all its faults and eccentricities his two-volume work is a masterpiece and a landmark, in his own words, 'setting the orthography, displaying the analogy, regulating the structures, and ascertaining the significations of English words'. It is the cornerstone of Standard English, an achievement which, in James Boswell's words, 'conferred stability on the language of his country'.

The *Dictionary*, together with his other writing, made Johnson famous and so well esteemed that his friends were able to prevail upon King George III to offer him a pension. From then on, he was to become the Johnson of folklore.

Questions 1–3

*Choose **THREE** letters A–H.*

Write your answers in boxes 1–3 on your answer sheet.

NB *Your answers may be given in any order.*

Which **THREE** of the following statements are true of Johnson's *Dictionary*?

    A   It avoided all scholarly words.

    B   It was the only English dictionary in general use for 200 years.

    C   It was famous because of the large number of people involved.

    D   It focused mainly on language from contemporary texts.

    E   There was a time limit for its completion.

    F   It ignored work done by previous dictionary writers.

    G   It took into account subtleties of meaning.

    H   Its definitions were famous for their originality.

Questions 4–7

Complete the summary.

*Choose **NO MORE THAN TWO WORDS** from the passage for each answer.*

Write your answers in boxes 4–7 on your answer sheet.

In 1764 Dr Johnson accepted the contract to produce a dictionary. Having rented a garret, he took on a number of **4** .... , who stood at a long central desk. Johnson did not have a **5** .... available to him, but eventually produced definitions of in excess of 40,000 words written down in 80 large notebooks. On publication, the *Dictionary* was immediately hailed in many European countries as a landmark. According to his biographer, James Boswell, Johnson's principal achievement was to bring **6** .... to the English language. As a reward for his hard work, he was granted a **7** .... by the king.

Questions 8–13

Do the following statements agree with the information given in Reading Passage 1?

In boxes 8–13 on your answer sheet, write

> **TRUE**　　　　*if the statement agrees with the information*
> **FALSE**　　　　*if the statement contradicts the information*
> **NOT GIVEN**　*if there is no information on this*

8　The growing importance of the middle classes led to an increased demand for dictionaries.

9　Johnson has become more well known since his death.

10　Johnson had been planning to write a dictionary for several years.

11　Johnson set up an academy to help with the writing of his *Dictionary*.

12　Johnson only received payment for his *Dictionary* on its completion.

13　Not all of the assistants survived to see the publication of the *Dictionary*.

READING PASSAGE 2

*You should spend about 20 minutes on **Questions 14–26**, which are based on Reading Passage 2 below.*

Nature or Nurture?

A   A few years ago, in one of the most fascinating and disturbing experiments in behavioural psychology, Stanley Milgram of Yale University tested 40 subjects from all walks of life for their willingness to obey instructions given by a 'leader' in a situation in which the subjects might feel a personal distaste for the actions they were called upon to perform. Specifically, Milgram told each volunteer 'teacher-subject' that the experiment was in the noble cause of education, and was designed to test whether or not punishing pupils for their mistakes would have a positive effect on the pupils' ability to learn.

B   Milgram's experimental set-up involved placing the teacher-subject before a panel of thirty switches with labels ranging from '15 volts of electricity (slight shock)' to '450 volts (danger – severe shock)' in steps of 15 volts each. The teacher-subject was told that whenever the pupil gave the wrong answer to a question, a shock was to be administered, beginning at the lowest level and increasing in severity with each successive wrong answer. The supposed 'pupil' was in reality an actor hired by Milgram to simulate receiving the shocks by emitting a spectrum of groans, screams and writhings together with an assortment of statements and expletives denouncing both the experiment and the experimenter. Milgram told the teacher-subject to ignore the reactions of the pupil, and to administer whatever level of shock was called for, as per the rule governing the experimental situation of the moment.

C   As the experiment unfolded, the pupil would deliberately give the wrong answers to questions posed by the teacher, thereby bringing on various electrical punishments, even up to the danger level of 300 volts and beyond. Many of the teacher-subjects balked at administering the higher levels of punishment, and turned to Milgram with questioning looks and/or complaints about continuing the experiment. In these situations, Milgram calmly explained that the teacher-subject was to ignore the pupil's cries for mercy and carry on with the experiment. If the subject was still reluctant to proceed, Milgram said that it was important for the sake of the experiment that the procedure be followed through to the end. His final argument was, 'You have no other choice. You must go on.' What Milgram was trying to discover was the number of teacher-subjects who would be willing to administer the highest levels of shock, even in the face of strong personal and moral revulsion against the rules and conditions of the experiment.

D   Prior to carrying out the experiment, Milgram explained his idea to a group of 39 psychiatrists and asked them to predict the average percentage of people in an ordinary population who would be willing to administer the highest shock level of 450 volts. The overwhelming consensus was that virtually all the teacher-subjects would refuse to obey the experimenter. The psychiatrists felt that 'most subjects would not go beyond 150 volts' and they further anticipated that only four per cent would go up to 300 volts.

Furthermore, they thought that only a lunatic fringe of about one in 1,000 would give the highest shock of 450 volts.

E   What were the actual results? Well, over 60 per cent of the teacher-subjects continued to obey Milgram up to the 450-volt limit! In repetitions of the experiment in other countries, the percentage of obedient teacher-subjects was even higher, reaching 85 per cent in one country. How can we possibly account for this vast discrepancy between what calm, rational, knowledgeable people predict in the comfort of their study and what pressured, flustered, but cooperative 'teachers' actually do in the laboratory of real life?

F   One's first inclination might be to argue that there must be some sort of built-in animal aggression instinct that was activated by the experiment, and that Milgram's teacher-subjects were just following a genetic need to discharge this pent-up primal urge onto the pupil by administering the electrical shock. A modern hard-core sociobiologist might even go so far as to claim that this aggressive instinct evolved as an advantageous trait, having been of survival value to our ancestors in their struggle against the hardships of life on the plains and in the caves, ultimately finding its way into our genetic make-up as a remnant of our ancient animal ways.

G   An alternative to this notion of genetic programming is to see the teacher-subjects' actions as a result of the social environment under which the experiment was carried out. As Milgram himself pointed out, 'Most subjects in the experiment see their behaviour in a larger context that is benevolent and useful to society – the pursuit of scientific truth. The psychological laboratory has a strong claim to legitimacy and evokes trust and confidence in those who perform there. An action such as shocking a victim, which in isolation appears evil, acquires a completely different meaning when placed in this setting.'

H   Thus, in this explanation the subject merges his unique personality and personal and moral code with that of larger institutional structures, surrendering individual properties like loyalty, self-sacrifice and discipline to the service of malevolent systems of authority.

I   Here we have two radically different explanations for why so many teacher-subjects were willing to forgo their sense of personal responsibility for the sake of an institutional authority figure. The problem for biologists, psychologists and anthropologists is to sort out which of these two polar explanations is more plausible. This, in essence, is the problem of modern sociobiology – to discover the degree to which hard-wired genetic programming dictates, or at least strongly biases, the interaction of animals and humans with their environment, that is, their behaviour. Put another way, sociobiology is concerned with elucidating the biological basis of all behaviour.

Questions 14–19

Reading Passage 2 has nine paragraphs, **A–I**.

Which paragraph contains the following information?

*Write the correct letter **A–I** in boxes 14–19 on your answer sheet.*

14   a biological explanation of the teacher-subjects' behaviour

15   the explanation Milgram gave the teacher-subjects for the experiment

16   the identity of the pupils

17   the expected statistical outcome

18   the general aim of sociobiological study

19   the way Milgram persuaded the teacher-subjects to continue

Questions 20–22

*Choose the correct letter, **A, B, C** or **D**.*

Write your answers in boxes 20–22 on your answer sheet.

20   The teacher-subjects were told that they were testing whether

    A   a 450-volt shock was dangerous.
    B   punishment helps learning.
    C   the pupils were honest.
    D   they were suited to teaching.

21   The teacher-subjects were instructed to

    A   stop when a pupil asked them to.
    B   denounce pupils who made mistakes.
    C   reduce the shock level after a correct answer.
    D   give punishment according to a rule.

22   Before the experiment took place the psychiatrists

    A   believed that a shock of 150 volts was too dangerous.
    B   failed to agree on how the teacher-subjects would respond to instructions.
    C   underestimated the teacher-subjects' willingness to comply with experimental procedure.
    D   thought that many of the teacher-subjects would administer a shock of 450 volts.

Questions 23–26

Do the following statements agree with the information given in Reading Passage 2?

In boxes 23–26 on your answer sheet, write

> **TRUE**   *if the statement agrees with the information*
> **FALSE**   *if the statement contradicts the information*
> **NOT GIVEN**   *if there is no information on this*

23   Several of the subjects were psychology students at Yale University.

24   Some people may believe that the teacher-subjects' behaviour could be explained as a positive survival mechanism.

25   In a sociological explanation, personal values are more powerful than authority.

26   Milgram's experiment solves an important question in sociobiology.

READING PASSAGE 3

*You should spend about 20 minutes on **Questions 27–40**, which are based on Reading Passage 3 below.*

The Truth about the Environment

For many environmentalists, the world seems to be getting worse. They have developed a hit-list of our main fears: that natural resources are running out; that the population is ever growing, leaving less and less to eat; that species are becoming extinct in vast numbers, and that the planet's air and water are becoming ever more polluted.

But a quick look at the facts shows a different picture. First, energy and other natural resources have become more abundant, not less so, since the book 'The Limits to Growth' was published in 1972 by a group of scientists. Second, more food is now produced per head of the world's population than at any time in history. Fewer people are starving. Third, although species are indeed becoming extinct, only about 0.7% of them are expected to disappear in the next 50 years, not 25–50%, as has so often been predicted. And finally, most forms of environmental pollution either appear to have been exaggerated, or are transient – associated with the early phases of industrialisation and therefore best cured not by restricting economic growth, but by accelerating it. One form of pollution – the release of greenhouse gases that causes global warming – does appear to be a phenomenon that is going to extend well into our future, but its total impact is unlikely to pose a devastating problem. A bigger problem may well turn out to be an inappropriate response to it.

Yet opinion polls suggest that many people nurture the belief that environmental standards are declining and four factors seem to cause this disjunction between perception and reality.

One is the lopsidedness built into scientific research. Scientific funding goes mainly to areas with many problems. That may be wise policy, but it will also create an impression that many more potential problems exist than is the case.

Secondly, environmental groups need to be noticed by the mass media. They also need to keep the money rolling in. Understandably, perhaps, they sometimes overstate their arguments. In 1997, for example, the World Wide Fund for Nature issued a press release entitled: 'Two thirds of the world's forests lost forever'. The truth turns out to be nearer 20%.

Though these groups are run overwhelmingly by selfless folk, they nevertheless share many of the characteristics of other lobby groups. That would matter less if people applied the same degree of scepticism to environmental lobbying as they do to lobby groups in other fields. A trade organisation arguing for, say, weaker pollution controls is instantly seen as self-interested. Yet a green organisation opposing such a weakening is seen as altruistic, even if an impartial view of the controls in question might suggest they are doing more harm than good.

A third source of confusion is the attitude of the media. People are clearly more curious about bad news than good. Newspapers and broadcasters are there to provide what the public wants. That, however, can lead to significant distortions of perception. An example was America's encounter with El Niño in 1997 and 1998. This climatic phenomenon was accused of wrecking tourism, causing allergies, melting the ski-slopes and causing 22 deaths. However, according to an article in the *Bulletin of the American Meteorological Society*, the damage it did was estimated at US$4 billion but the benefits amounted to some US$19 billion. These came from higher winter temperatures (which saved an estimated 850 lives, reduced heating costs and diminished spring floods caused by meltwaters).

The fourth factor is poor individual perception. People worry that the endless rise in the amount of stuff everyone throws away will cause the world to run out of places to dispose of waste. Yet, even if America's trash output continues to rise as it has done in the past, and even if the American population doubles by 2100, all the rubbish America produces through the entire 21st century will still take up only one-12,000th of the area of the entire United States.

So what of global warming? As we know, carbon dioxide emissions are causing the planet to warm. The best estimates are that the temperatures will rise by 2–3°C in this century, causing considerable problems, at a total cost of US$5,000 billion.

Despite the intuition that something drastic needs to be done about such a costly problem, economic analyses clearly show it will be far more expensive to cut carbon dioxide emissions radically than to pay the costs of adaptation to the increased temperatures. A model by one of the main authors of the United Nations Climate Change Panel shows how an expected temperature increase of 2.1 degrees in 2100 would only be diminished to an increase of 1.9 degrees. Or to put it another way, the temperature increase that the planet would have experienced in 2094 would be postponed to 2100.

So this does not prevent global warming, but merely buys the world six years. Yet the cost of reducing carbon dioxide emissions, for the United States alone, will be higher than the cost of solving the world's single, most pressing health problem: providing universal access to clean drinking water and sanitation. Such measures would avoid 2 million deaths every year, and prevent half a billion people from becoming seriously ill.

It is crucial that we look at the facts if we want to make the best possible decisions for the future. It may be costly to be overly optimistic – but more costly still to be too pessimistic.

Questions 27–32

Do the following statements agree with the claims of the writer in Reading Passage 3?

In boxes 27–32 on your answer sheet, write

YES	*if the statement agrees with the writer's claims*
NO	*if the statement contradicts the writer's claims*
NOT GIVEN	*if it is impossible to say what the writer thinks about this*

27 Environmentalists take a pessimistic view of the world for a number of reasons.

28 Data on the Earth's natural resources has only been collected since 1972.

29 The number of starving people in the world has increased in recent years.

30 Extinct species are being replaced by new species.

31 Some pollution problems have been correctly linked to industrialisation.

32 It would be best to attempt to slow down economic growth.

Questions 33–37

*Choose the correct letter, **A**, **B**, **C** or **D**.*

Write your answers in boxes 33–37 on your answer sheet.

33 What aspect of scientific research does the writer express concern about in paragraph 4?

    A the need to produce results
    B the lack of financial support
    C the selection of areas to research
    D the desire to solve every research problem

34 The writer quotes from the Worldwide Fund for Nature to illustrate how

    A influential the mass media can be.
    B effective environmental groups can be.
    C the mass media can help groups raise funds.
    D environmental groups can exaggerate their claims.

35 What is the writer's main point about lobby groups in paragraph 6?

    A Some are more active than others.
    B Some are better organised than others.
    C Some receive more criticism than others.
    D Some support more important issues than others.

36 The writer suggests that newspapers print items that are intended to

    A educate readers.
    B meet their readers' expectations.
    C encourage feedback from readers.
    D mislead readers.

37 What does the writer say about America's waste problem?

    A It will increase in line with population growth.
    B It is not as important as we have been led to believe.
    C It has been reduced through public awareness of the issues.
    D It is only significant in certain areas of the country.

Questions 38–40

Complete the summary with the list of words A–I below.

Write the correct letter A–I in boxes 38–40 on your answer sheet.

GLOBAL WARMING

The writer admits that global warming is a **38** .... challenge, but says that it will not have a catastrophic impact on our future, if we deal with it in the **39** .... way. If we try to reduce the levels of greenhouse gases, he believes that it would only have a minimal impact on rising temperatures. He feels it would be better to spend money on the more **40** .... health problem of providing the world's population with clean drinking water.

A unrealistic	**B** agreed	**C** expensive	**D** right
E long-term	**F** usual	**G** surprising	**H** personal
I urgent			

WRITING

WRITING TASK 1

You should spend about 20 minutes on this task.

> *The graph below shows the proportion of the population aged 65 and over between 1940 and 2040 in three different countries.*
>
> *Summarise the information by selecting and reporting the main features, and make comparisons where relevant.*

Write at least 150 words.

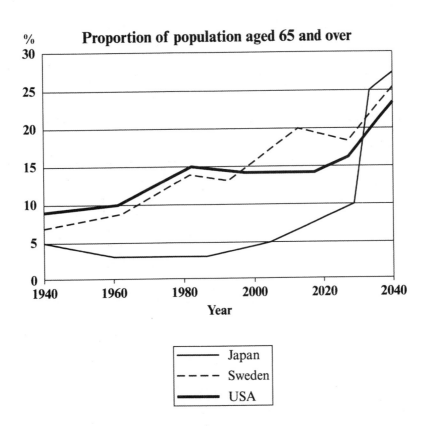

WRITING TASK 2

You should spend about 40 minutes on this task.

Write about the following topic:

> **Universities should accept equal numbers of male and female students in every subject.**
>
> **To what extent do you agree or disagree?**

Give reasons for your answer and include any relevant examples from your own knowledge or experience.

Write at least 250 words.

SPEAKING

PART 1

The examiner asks the candidate about him/herself, his/her home, work or studies and other familiar topics.

EXAMPLE

Your country

- Which part of your country do most people live in?
- Tell me about the main industries there.
- How easy is it to travel around your country?
- Has your country changed much since you were a child?

PART 2

> **Describe a well-known person you like or admire.**
>
> **You should say:**
>   **who this person is**
>   **what this person has done**
>   **why this person is well known**
> **and explain why you admire this person.**

You will have to talk about the topic for one to two minutes.
You have one minute to think about what you're going to say.
You can make some notes to help you if you wish.

PART 3

Discussion topics:

Famous people in your country

Example questions:
What kind of people become famous people these days?
Is this different from the kind of achievement that made people famous in the past?
In what way?
How do you think people will become famous in the future?

Being in the public eye

Example questions:
What are the good things about being famous? Are there any disadvantages?
How does the media in your country treat famous people?
Why do you think ordinary people are interested in the lives of famous people?

Test 2

SECTION 1   *Questions 1–10*

Questions 1–10

Complete the notes below.

*Write **NO MORE THAN THREE WORDS AND/OR A NUMBER** for each answer.*

LIBRARY INFORMATION

Example	*Answer*
Minimum joining age:	18 years

For registration, must take

- two **1** .... and
- two forms of I.D. e.g. driving licence, **2** ....

Cost to join per year (without current student card): **3** £ ....
Number of items allowed: (members of public) **4** ....
Loan times: four weeks
Fines start at **5** £ ....
Computers can be booked up to **6** .... hours in advance
Library holds most national papers, all **7** .... , and magazines
Need **8** .... to use photocopier

Creative Writing class

- tutor is John **9** ....
- held on **10** .... evenings

SECTION 2   *Questions 11–20*

Questions 11–15

Choose the correct letter, A, B or C.

BICYCLES FOR THE WORLD

11 In 1993 Dan Pearman went to Ecuador

    A   as a tourist guide.
    B   as part of his studies.
    C   as a voluntary worker.

12 Dan's neighbour was successful in business because he

    A   employed carpenters from the area.
    B   was the most skilled craftsman in the town.
    C   found it easy to reach customers.

13 Dan says the charity relies on

    A   getting enough bicycles to send regularly.
    B   finding new areas which need the bicycles.
    C   charging for the bicycles it sends abroad.

14 What does Dan say about the town of Rivas?

    A   It has received the greatest number of bikes.
    B   It has almost as many bikes as Amsterdam.
    C   Its economy has been totally transformed.

15 What problem did the charity face in August 2000?

    A   It couldn't meet its overheads.
    B   It had to delay sending the bikes.
    C   It was criticised in the British media.

Questions 16 and 17

Answer the questions below.

*Write **NO MORE THAN ONE WORD OR A NUMBER** for each answer.*

16 How much money did the charity receive when it won an award?

....

17 What is the charity currently hoping to buy?

....

Questions 18–20

*Choose **THREE** letters A–G.*

*Which **THREE** things can the general public do to help the charity Pedal Power?*

A	organise a bicycle collection
B	repair the donated bikes
C	donate their unwanted tools
D	do voluntary work in its office
E	hold an event to raise money
F	identify areas that need bikes
G	write to the government

SECTION 3   *Questions 21–30*

Questions 21–30

Complete the table below.

*Write **NO MORE THAN THREE WORDS AND/OR A NUMBER** for each answer.*

'Student Life' video project		
	Cristina	Ibrahim
Enjoyed:	• using the camera • going to a British **21**	contact with students doing other courses (has asked some to **22** .... with him)
Most useful language practice:	• listening to instructions • learning **23** .... vocabulary	listening to British students' language because of: – normal speed – large amount of **24** ....

General usefulness:	• operating video camera
	• working with other people:
	  – learning about
	    25 ....
	  – compromising
	  – **26** .... people who have different views
		the importance of
		27 ....

Things to do differently in future:	• decide when to
	  28 .... each stage at the beginning
	• make more effort to
	  29 .... with the camera
		don't make the film too
		30 ....

SECTION 4   *Questions 31–40*

Questions 31–40

Complete the notes below.

*Write **NO MORE THAN THREE WORDS AND/OR A NUMBER** for each answer.*

ANTARCTICA

GEOGRAPHY

- world's highest, coldest and windiest continent
- more than **31** .... times as big as the UK
- most of the area is classified as **32** ....

RESEARCH STATIONS

- international teams work together
- **33** .... is integrated with technical support
- stations contain accommodation, work areas, a kitchen, a **34** .... and a gym
- supplies were brought to Zero One station by sledge from a **35** .... at the edge of the ice 15 km away
- problem of snow build-ups solved by building stations on **36** .... with adjustable legs

FOOD AND DIET

- average daily requirement for an adult in Antarctica is approximately **37** .... kilocalories
- rations for field work prepared by process of freeze-drying

---

RESEARCH

The most important research focuses on climate change, including
- measuring changes in the ice-cap (because of effects on sea levels and
  38 ....)
- monitoring the hole in the ozone layer
- analysing air from bubbles in ice to measure **39** .... caused by human activity

WORK OPPORTUNITIES

Many openings for **40** .... people including
- research assistants
- administrative and technical positions

READING

READING PASSAGE 1

*You should spend about 20 minutes on **Questions 1–13**, which are based on Reading Passage 1 below.*

BAKELITE

The birth of modern plastics

In 1907, Leo Hendrick Baekeland, a Belgian scientist working in New York, discovered and patented a revolutionary new synthetic material. His invention, which he named 'Bakelite', was of enormous technological importance, and effectively launched the modern plastics industry.

The term 'plastic' comes from the Greek *plassein*, meaning 'to mould'. Some plastics are derived from natural sources, some are semi-synthetic (the result of chemical action on a natural substance), and some are entirely synthetic, that is, chemically engineered from the constituents of coal or oil. Some are 'thermoplastic', which means that, like candlewax, they melt when heated and can then be reshaped. Others are 'thermosetting': like eggs, they cannot revert to their original viscous state, and their shape is thus fixed for ever. Bakelite had the distinction of being the first totally synthetic thermosetting plastic.

The history of today's plastics begins with the discovery of a series of semi-synthetic thermoplastic materials in the mid-nineteenth century. The impetus behind the development of these early plastics was generated by a number of factors – immense technological progress in the domain of chemistry, coupled with wider cultural changes, and the pragmatic need to find acceptable substitutes for dwindling supplies of 'luxury' materials such as tortoiseshell and ivory.

Baekeland's interest in plastics began in 1885 when, as a young chemistry student in Belgium, he embarked on research into phenolic resins, the group of sticky substances produced when phenol (carbolic acid) combines with an aldehyde (a volatile fluid similar to alcohol). He soon abandoned the subject, however, only returning to it some years later. By 1905 he was a wealthy New Yorker, having recently made his fortune with the invention of a new photographic paper. While Baekeland had been busily amassing dollars, some advances had been made in the development of plastics. The years 1899 and 1900 had seen the patenting of the first semi-synthetic thermosetting material that could be manufactured on an industrial scale. In purely scientific terms, Baekeland's major contribution to the field is not so much the actual discovery of the material to which he gave his name, but rather the method by which a reaction between phenol and formaldehyde could be controlled, thus making possible its preparation on a commercial basis. On 13 July 1907, Baekeland took out his famous patent describing this preparation, the essential features of which are still in use today.

The original patent outlined a three-stage process, in which phenol and formaldehyde (from wood or coal) were initially combined under vacuum inside a large egg-shaped kettle. The result was a resin known as Novalak, which became soluble and malleable when heated. The resin was allowed to cool in shallow trays until it hardened, and then broken up and ground into powder. Other substances were then introduced: including fillers, such as woodflour, asbestos or cotton, which increase strength and moisture resistance, catalysts (substances to speed up the reaction between two chemicals without joining to either) and hexa, a compound of ammonia and formaldehyde which supplied the additional formaldehyde necessary to form a thermosetting resin. This resin was then left to cool and harden, and ground up a second time. The resulting granular powder was raw Bakelite, ready to be made into a vast range of manufactured objects. In the last stage, the heated Bakelite was poured into a hollow mould of the required shape and subjected to extreme heat and pressure, thereby 'setting' its form for life.

The design of Bakelite objects, everything from earrings to television sets, was governed to a large extent by the technical requirements of the moulding process. The object could not be designed so that it was locked into the mould and therefore difficult to extract. A common general rule was that objects should taper towards the deepest part of the mould, and if necessary the product was moulded in separate pieces. Moulds had to be carefully designed so that the molten Bakelite would flow evenly and completely into the mould. Sharp corners proved impractical and were thus avoided, giving rise to the smooth, 'streamlined' style popular in the 1930s. The thickness of the walls of the mould was also crucial: thick walls took longer to cool and harden, a factor which had to be considered by the designer in order to make the most efficient use of machines.

Baekeland's invention, although treated with disdain in its early years, went on to enjoy an unparalleled popularity which lasted throughout the first half of the twentieth century. It became the wonder product of the new world of industrial expansion – 'the material of a thousand uses'. Being both non-porous and heat-resistant, Bakelite kitchen goods were promoted as being germ-free and sterilisable. Electrical manufacturers seized on its insulating properties, and consumers everywhere relished its dazzling array of shades, delighted that they were now, at last, no longer restricted to the wood tones and drab browns of the pre-plastic era. It then fell from favour again during the 1950s, and was despised and destroyed in vast quantities. Recently, however, it has been experiencing something of a renaissance, with renewed demand for original Bakelite objects in the collectors' marketplace, and museums, societies and dedicated individuals once again appreciating the style and originality of this innovative material.

Questions 1–3

Complete the summary.

*Choose **ONE WORD ONLY** from the passage for each answer.*

Write your answers in boxes 1–3 on your answer sheet.

Some plastics behave in a similar way to **1** .... in that they melt under heat and can be moulded into new forms. Bakelite was unique because it was the first material to be both entirely **2** .... in origin, and thermosetting.

There were several reasons for the research into plastics in the nineteenth century, among them the great advances that had been made in the field of **3** .... and the search for alternatives to natural resources like ivory.

Questions 4–8

Complete the flow-chart.

*Choose **ONE WORD ONLY** from the passage for each answer.*

Write your answers in boxes 4–8 on your answer sheet.

The Production of Bakelite

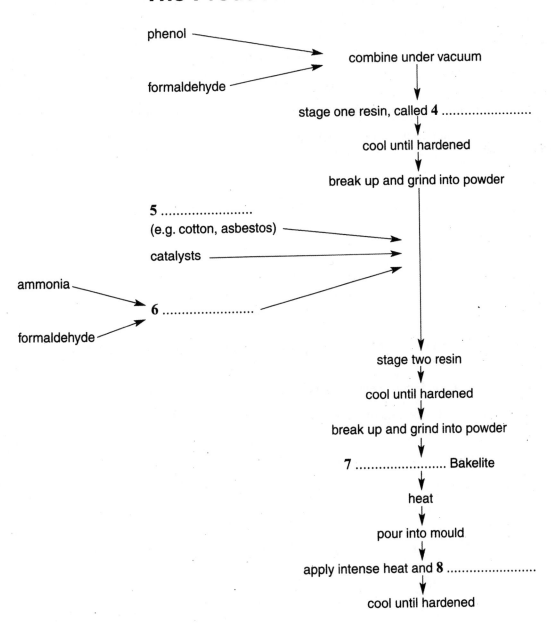

phenol ⟶

formaldehyde ⟶

combine under vacuum

↓

stage one resin, called **4** ....

↓

cool until hardened

↓

break up and grind into powder

5 ....
(e.g. cotton, asbestos) ⟶

catalysts ⟶

ammonia ⟶

formaldehyde ⟶

6 .... ⟶

↓

stage two resin

↓

cool until hardened

↓

break up and grind into powder

↓

7 .... Bakelite

↓

heat

↓

pour into mould

↓

apply intense heat and **8** ....

↓

cool until hardened

Questions 9 and 10

Choose **TWO** *letters A–E.*

Write your answers in boxes 9 and 10 on your answer sheet.

NB   Your answers may be given in either order.

Which **TWO** of the following factors influencing the design of Bakelite objects are mentioned in the text?

    A   the function which the object would serve

    B   the ease with which the resin could fill the mould

    C   the facility with which the object could be removed from the mould

    D   the limitations of the materials used to manufacture the mould

    E   the fashionable styles of the period

Questions 11–13

Do the following statements agree with the information given in Reading Passage 1?

In boxes 11–13 on your answer sheet, write

    TRUE   *if the statement agrees with the information*
    FALSE   *if the statement contradicts the information*
    NOT GIVEN   *if there is no information on this*

11   Modern-day plastic preparation is based on the same principles as that patented in 1907.

12   Bakelite was immediately welcomed as a practical and versatile material.

13   Bakelite was only available in a limited range of colours.

READING PASSAGE 2

*You should spend about 20 minutes on **Questions 14–27**, which are based on Reading Passage 2 below.*

What's so funny?

John McCrone reviews recent research on humour

The joke comes over the headphones: 'Which side of a dog has the most hair? The left.' No, not funny. Try again. 'Which side of a dog has the most hair? The outside.' Hah! The punchline is silly yet fitting, tempting a smile, even a laugh. Laughter has always struck people as deeply mysterious, perhaps pointless. The writer Arthur Koestler dubbed it the luxury reflex: 'unique in that it serves no apparent biological purpose'.

Theories about humour have an ancient pedigree. Plato expressed the idea that humour is simply a delighted feeling of superiority over others. Kant and Freud felt that joke-telling relies on building up a psychic tension which is safely punctured by the ludicrousness of the punchline. But most modern humour theorists have settled on some version of Aristotle's belief that jokes are based on a reaction to or resolution of incongruity, when the punchline is either a nonsense or, though appearing silly, has a clever second meaning.

Graeme Ritchie, a computational linguist in Edinburgh, studies the linguistic structure of jokes in order to understand not only humour but language understanding and reasoning in machines. He says that while there is no single format for jokes, many revolve around a sudden and surprising conceptual shift. A comedian will present a situation followed by an unexpected interpretation that is also apt.

So even if a punchline sounds silly, the listener can see there is a clever semantic fit and that sudden mental 'Aha!' is the buzz that makes us laugh. Viewed from this angle, humour is just a form of creative insight, a sudden leap to a new perspective.

However, there is another type of laughter, the laughter of social appeasement and it is important to understand this too. Play is a crucial part of development in most young mammals. Rats produce ultrasonic squeaks to prevent their scuffles turning nasty. Chimpanzees have a 'play-face' – a gaping expression accompanied by a panting 'ah, ah' noise. In humans, these signals have mutated into smiles and laughs. Researchers believe social situations, rather than cognitive events such as jokes, trigger these instinctual markers of play or appeasement. People laugh on fairground rides or when tickled to flag a play situation, whether they feel amused or not.

Both social and cognitive types of laughter tap into the same expressive machinery in our brains, the emotion and motor circuits that produce smiles and excited vocalisations. However, if cognitive laughter is the product of more general thought processes, it should result from more expansive brain activity.

Psychologist Vinod Goel investigated humour using the new technique of 'single event' functional magnetic resonance imaging (fMRI). An MRI scanner uses magnetic fields and radio waves to track the changes in oxygenated blood that accompany mental activity. Until recently, MRI scanners needed several minutes of activity and so could not be used to track rapid thought processes such as comprehending a joke. New developments now allow half-second 'snapshots' of all sorts of reasoning and problem-solving activities.

Although Goel felt being inside a brain scanner was hardly the ideal place for appreciating a joke, he found evidence that understanding a joke involves a widespread mental shift. His scans showed that at the beginning of a joke the listener's prefrontal cortex lit up, particularly the right prefrontal believed to be critical for problem solving. But there was also activity in the temporal lobes at the side of the head (consistent with attempts to rouse stored knowledge) and in many other brain areas. Then when the punchline arrived, a new area sprang to life – the orbital prefrontal cortex. This patch of brain tucked behind the orbits of the eyes is associated with evaluating information.

Making a rapid emotional assessment of the events of the moment is an extremely demanding job for the brain, animal or human. Energy and arousal levels may need to be retuned in the blink of an eye. These abrupt changes will produce either positive or negative feelings. The orbital cortex, the region that becomes active in Goel's experiment, seems the best candidate for the site that feeds such feelings into higher-level thought processes, with its close connections to the brain's sub-cortical arousal apparatus and centres of metabolic control.

All warm-blooded animals make constant tiny adjustments in arousal in response to external events, but humans, who have developed a much more complicated internal life as a result of language, respond emotionally not only to their surroundings, but to their own thoughts. Whenever a sought-for answer snaps into place, there is a shudder of pleased recognition. Creative discovery being pleasurable, humans have learned to find ways of milking this natural response. The fact that jokes tap into our general evaluative machinery explains why the line between funny and disgusting, or funny and frightening, can be so fine. Whether a joke gives pleasure or pain depends on a person's outlook.

Humour may be a luxury, but the mechanism behind it is no evolutionary accident. As Peter Derks, a psychologist at William and Mary College in Virginia, says: 'I like to think of humour as the distorted mirror of the mind. It's creative, perceptual, analytical and lingual. If we can figure out how the mind processes humour, then we'll have a pretty good handle on how it works in general.'

❖

Questions 14–20

Do the following statements agree with the information given in Reading Passage 2?

In boxes 14–20 on your answer sheet, write

>   **TRUE**   *if the statement agrees with the information*
>   **FALSE**   *if the statement contradicts the information*
>   **NOT GIVEN**   *if there is no information on this*

14   Arthur Koestler considered laughter biologically important in several ways.

15   Plato believed humour to be a sign of above-average intelligence.

16   Kant believed that a successful joke involves the controlled release of nervous energy.

17   Current thinking on humour has largely ignored Aristotle's view on the subject.

18   Graeme Ritchie's work links jokes to artificial intelligence.

19   Most comedians use personal situations as a source of humour.

20   Chimpanzees make particular noises when they are playing.

Questions 21–23

The diagram below shows the areas of the brain activated by jokes.

Label the diagram.

Choose **NO MORE THAN TWO WORDS** *from the passage for each answer.*

Write your answers in boxes 21–23 on your answer sheet.

Right prefrontal cortex lights
up – area of brain linked to
21 ....

Orbital prefrontal cortex is
activated – involved with
23 ....

22 .... become
active too

Questions 24–27

*Complete each sentence with the correct ending **A–G** below.*

*Write the correct letter **A–G** in boxes 24–27 on your answer sheet.*

24 One of the brain's most difficult tasks is to

25 Because of the language they have developed, humans

26 Individual responses to humour

27 Peter Derks believes that humour

A	react to their own thoughts.
B	helped create language in humans.
C	respond instantly to whatever is happening.
D	may provide valuable information about the operation of the brain.
E	cope with difficult situations.
F	relate to a person's subjective views.
G	led our ancestors to smile and then laugh.

READING PASSAGE 3

*You should spend about 20 minutes on **Questions 28–40**, which are based on Reading Passage 3 below.*

The Birth of Scientific English

World science is dominated today by a small number of languages, including Japanese, German and French, but it is English which is probably the most popular global language of science. This is not just because of the importance of English-speaking countries such as the USA in scientific research; the scientists of many non-English-speaking countries find that they need to write their research papers in English to reach a wide international audience. Given the prominence of scientific English today, it may seem surprising that no one really knew *how* to write science in English before the 17th century. Before that, Latin was regarded as the *lingua franca*[1] for European intellectuals.

The European Renaissance (c. 14th–16th century) is sometimes called the 'revival of learning', a time of renewed interest in the 'lost knowledge' of classical times. At the same time, however, scholars also began to test and extend this knowledge. The emergent nation states of Europe developed competitive interests in world exploration and the development of trade. Such expansion, which was to take the English language west to America and east to India, was supported by scientific developments such as the discovery of magnetism (and hence the invention of the compass), improvements in cartography and – perhaps the most important scientific revolution of them all – the new theories of astronomy and the movement of the Earth in relation to the planets and stars, developed by Copernicus (1473–1543).

England was one of the first countries where scientists adopted and publicised Copernican ideas with enthusiasm. Some of these scholars, including two with interests in language – John Wallis and John Wilkins – helped found the Royal Society in 1660 in order to promote empirical scientific research.

Across Europe similar academies and societies arose, creating new national traditions of science. In the initial stages of the scientific revolution, most publications in the national languages were popular works, encyclopaedias, educational textbooks and translations. Original science was not done in English until the second half of the 17th century. For example, Newton published his mathematical treatise, known as the *Principia*, in Latin, but published his later work on the properties of light – *Opticks* – in English.

There were several reasons why original science continued to be written in Latin. The first was simply a matter of audience. Latin was suitable for an international audience of scholars, whereas English reached a socially wider, but more local, audience. Hence, popular science was written in English.

[1] *lingua franca*: a language which is used for communication between groups of people who speak different languages

A second reason for writing in Latin may, perversely, have been a concern for secrecy. Open publication had dangers in putting into the public domain preliminary ideas which had not yet been fully exploited by their 'author'. This growing concern about intellectual property rights was a feature of the period – it reflected both the humanist notion of the individual, rational scientist who invents and discovers through private intellectual labour, and the growing connection between original science and commercial exploitation. There was something of a social distinction between 'scholars and gentlemen' who understood Latin, and men of trade who lacked a classical education. And in the mid-17th century it was common practice for mathematicians to keep their discoveries and proofs secret, by writing them in cipher, in obscure languages, or in private messages deposited in a sealed box with the Royal Society. Some scientists might have felt more comfortable with Latin precisely because its audience, though international, was socially restricted. Doctors clung the most keenly to Latin as an 'insider language'.

A third reason why the writing of original science in English was delayed may have been to do with the linguistic inadequacy of English in the early modern period. English was not well equipped to deal with scientific argument. First, it lacked the necessary technical vocabulary. Second, it lacked the grammatical resources required to represent the world in an objective and impersonal way, and to discuss the relations, such as cause and effect, that might hold between complex and hypothetical entities.

Fortunately, several members of the Royal Society possessed an interest in language and became engaged in various linguistic projects. Although a proposal in 1664 to establish a committee for improving the English language came to little, the society's members did a great deal to foster the publication of science in English and to encourage the development of a suitable writing style. Many members of the Royal Society also published monographs in English. One of the first was by Robert Hooke, the society's first curator of experiments, who described his experiments with microscopes in *Micrographia* (1665). This work is largely narrative in style, based on a transcript of oral demonstrations and lectures.

In 1665 a new scientific journal, *Philosophical Transactions*, was inaugurated. Perhaps the first international English-language scientific journal, it encouraged a new genre of scientific writing, that of short, focused accounts of particular experiments.

The 17th century was thus a formative period in the establishment of scientific English. In the following century much of this momentum was lost as German established itself as the leading European language of science. It is estimated that by the end of the 18th century 401 German scientific journals had been established as opposed to 96 in France and 50 in England. However, in the 19th century scientific English again enjoyed substantial lexical growth as the industrial revolution created the need for new technical vocabulary, and new, specialised, professional societies were instituted to promote and publish in the new disciplines.

Questions 28–34

Complete the summary.

*Choose **NO MORE THAN TWO WORDS** from the passage for each answer.*

Write your answers in boxes 28–34 on your answer sheet.

In Europe, modern science emerged at the same time as the nation state. At first, the scientific language of choice remained **28** .... It allowed scientists to communicate with other socially privileged thinkers while protecting their work from unwanted exploitation. Sometimes the desire to protect ideas seems to have been stronger than the desire to communicate them, particularly in the case of mathematicians and **29** .... In Britain, moreover, scientists worried that English had neither the **30** .... nor the **31** .... to express their ideas. This situation only changed after 1660 when scientists associated with the **32** .... set about developing English. An early scientific journal fostered a new kind of writing based on short descriptions of specific experiments. Although English was then overtaken by **33** .... , it developed again in the 19th century as a direct result of the **34** ....

Questions 35–37

Do the following statements agree with the information given in Reading Passage 3?

In boxes 35–37 on your answer sheet, write

TRUE	*if the statement agrees with the information*
FALSE	*if the statement contradicts the information*
NOT GIVEN	*if there is no information on this*

35 There was strong competition between scientists in Renaissance Europe.

36 The most important scientific development of the Renaissance period was the discovery of magnetism.

37 In 17th-century Britain, leading thinkers combined their interest in science with an interest in how to express ideas.

Questions 38–40

Complete the table.

Choose **NO MORE THAN TWO WORDS** *from the passage for each answer.*

Write your answers in boxes 38–40 on your answer sheet.

Science written in the first half of the 17th century		
Language used	Latin	English
Type of science	Original	38 ....
Examples	39	Encyclopaedias
Target audience	International scholars	40 .... , but socially wider

WRITING

WRITING TASK 1

You should spend about 20 minutes on this task.

> *The charts below show the main reasons for study among students of different age groups and the amount of support they received from employers.*
>
> *Summarise the information by selecting and reporting the main features, and make comparisons where relevant.*

Write at least 150 words.

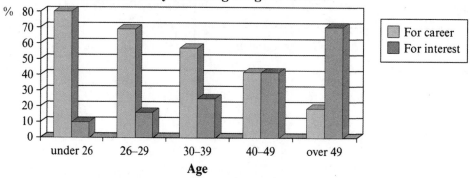

Reasons for study according to age of student

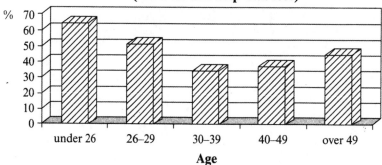

Employer support, by age group
(Time off and help with fees)

WRITING TASK 2

You should spend about 40 minutes on this task.

Write about the following topic:

> *In some countries young people are encouraged to work or travel for a year between finishing high school and starting university studies.*
>
> *Discuss the advantages and disadvantages for young people who decide to do this.*

Give reasons for your answer and include any relevant examples from your own knowledge or experience.

Write at least 250 words.

SPEAKING

PART 1

The examiner asks the candidate about him/herself, his/her home, work or studies and other familiar topics.

EXAMPLE

Colour

- What's your favourite colour? [Why?]
- Do you like the same colours now as you did when you were younger? [Why/Why not?]
- What can you learn about a person from the colours they like?
- Do any colours have a special meaning in your culture?

PART 2

> **Describe a song or a piece of music you like.**
>
> **You should say:**
>   **what the song or music is**
>   **what kind of song or music it is**
>   **where you first heard it**
> **and explain why you like it.**

You will have to talk about the topic for one to two minutes.

You have one minute to think about what you're going to say.

You can make some notes to help you if you wish.

PART 3

Discussion topics:

Music and young people

Example questions:
What kinds of music are popular with young people in your culture?
What do you think influences a young person's taste in music?
How has technology affected the kinds of music popular with young people?

Music and society

Example questions:
Tell me about any traditional music in your culture.
How important is it for a culture to have musical traditions?
Why do you think countries have national anthems or songs?

Test 3

SECTION 1   Questions 1–10

Questions 1–10

Complete the form below.

*Write **NO MORE THAN THREE WORDS AND/OR A NUMBER** for each answer.*

MINTONS CAR MART
Customer Enquiry

Example	*Answer*

Make: Lida
....

Engine size: 1 ....

Model: Max

Type of gears: 2 ....

Preferred colour: 3 .... blue

FINANCE

Customer wishes to arrange 4 ....

Part exchange? yes

PERSONAL DETAILS

Name: Wendy 5 ....

Title: 6 ....

Address: 20, Green Banks

7 ....

Hampshire

Postcode: GU8 9EW

Contact number: 8 (for .... only) 0798 257643

CURRENT CAR

Make: Conti

Model: Name: **9** ....

Year: 1994

Mileage: maximum 70,000

Colour: metallic grey

Condition: **10** ....

SECTION 2   *Questions 11–20*

Questions 11 and 12

Choose TWO letters A–E.

What **TWO** advantages does the speaker say Rexford University has for the students he is speaking to?

    A   higher than average results in examinations

    B   good transport links with central London

    C   near London Airport

    D   special government funding

    E   good links with local industry

Questions 13–15

Complete the notes below.

Write NO MORE THAN ONE WORD for each answer.

- When application is received, confirmation will be sent
- Application processing may be slowed down by
  - postal problems
  - delays in sending **13** ....
- University tries to put international applicants in touch with a student from the same **14** .... who can give information and advice on
  - academic atmosphere
  - leisure facilities
  - English **15** .... and food
  - what to pack

Questions 16–20

Choose the correct letter, A, B or C.

16 The speaker says international students at UK universities will be

    A   offered accommodation with local families.
    B   given special help by their lecturers.
    C   expected to work independently.

17 What does the speaker say about university accommodation on campus?

    A   Most places are given to undergraduates.
    B   No places are available for postgraduates with families.
    C   A limited number of places are available for new postgraduates.

18 Students wishing to live off-campus should apply

    A   several months in advance.
    B   two or three weeks in advance.
    C   at the beginning of term.

19 The university accommodation officer will

    A   send a list of agents for students to contact.
    B   contact accommodation agencies for students.
    C   ensure that students have suitable accommodation.

20 With regard to their English, the speaker advises the students to

    A   tell their lecturers if they have problems understanding.
    B   have private English lessons when they arrive.
    C   practise their spoken English before they arrive.

SECTION 3   *Questions 21–30*

Complete the form below.

Write **NO MORE THAN THREE WORDS AND/OR A NUMBER** *for each answer.*

Feedback Form

Course: *Communication in Business*

Course code: *CB162*

Dates: *From 21* .... *to 22* ....

Please give your comments on the following aspects of the course:

	Good Points	**Suggestions for Improvement**
Course organisation	• **23** .... • *useful to have* **24** .... *at beginning of course*	• *too much work in* **25** .... *of the course – could be more evenly balanced*
Course delivery	• *good* **26**	• *some* **27** .... *sessions went on too long*
Materials and equipment	• *good* **28**	• *not enough copies of key texts available* • *need more computers*
Testing and evaluation	• *quick feedback from oral presentations* • *marking criteria for oral presentations known in advance*	• *too much* **29** .... • *can we know criteria for marking final exams?*
Other comments	• *excellent* **30**	

SECTION 4   *Questions 31–40*

Questions 31–35

Complete the sentences below.

*Write **NO MORE THAN TWO WORDS AND/OR A NUMBER** for each answer.*

HOUSEHOLD WASTE RECYCLING

31   By 2008, carbon dioxide emissions need to be .... lower than in 1990.

32   Recycling saves energy and reduces emissions from landfill sites and ....

33   People say that one problem is a lack of '........................' sites for household waste.

•   At the 'bring banks', household waste is sorted and unsuitable items removed.

34   Glass designed to be utilised for .... cannot be recycled with other types of glass.

35   In the UK, ... tons of glass is recycled each year.

Questions 36–40

Complete the table below.

Write **NO MORE THAN TWO WORDS** *for each answer.*

Companies working with recycled materials		
Material	**Company**	**Product that the company manufactures**
glass	CLF Aggregates	*material used for making* **36** ....
paper	Martin's	*office stationery*
	Papersave	**37** .... *for use on farms*
plastic	Pacrite	**38** .... *for collecting waste*
	Waterford	**39** ....
	Johnson & Jones	**40** ....

READING

READING PASSAGE 1

*You should spend about 20 minutes on **Questions 1–13**, which are based on Reading Passage 1 below.*

Early Childhood Education

New Zealand's National Party spokesman on education, Dr Lockwood Smith, recently visited the US and Britain. Here he reports on the findings of his trip and what they could mean for New Zealand's education policy

A

'Education To Be More' was published last August. It was the report of the New Zealand Government's Early Childhood Care and Education Working Group. The report argued for enhanced equity of access and better funding for childcare and early childhood education institutions. Unquestionably, that's a real need; but since parents don't normally send children to pre-schools until the age of three, are we missing out on the most important years of all?

B

A 13-year study of early childhood development at Harvard University has shown that, by the age of three, most children have the potential to understand about 1000 words – most of the language they will use in ordinary conversation for the rest of their lives.

Furthermore, research has shown that while every child is born with a natural curiosity, it can be suppressed dramatically during the second and third years of life. Researchers claim that the human personality is formed during the first two years of life, and during the first three years children learn the basic skills they will use in all their later learning both at home and at school. Once over the age of three, children continue to expand on existing knowledge of the world.

C

It is generally acknowledged that young people from poorer socio-economic backgrounds tend to do less well in our education system. That's observed not just in New Zealand, but also in Australia, Britain and America. In an attempt to overcome that educational under-achievement, a nationwide programme called 'Headstart' was launched in the United States in 1965. A lot of money was poured into it. It took children into pre-school institutions at the age of three and was supposed to help the children of poorer families succeed in school.

Despite substantial funding, results have been disappointing. It is thought that there are two explanations for this. First, the programme began too late. Many children who entered it at the age of three were already behind their peers in language and measurable intelligence. Second, the parents were not involved. At the end of each day, 'Headstart' children returned to the same disadvantaged home environment.

D

As a result of the growing research evidence of the importance of the first three years of a child's life and the disappointing results from 'Headstart', a pilot programme was launched in Missouri in the US that focused on parents as the child's first teachers. The 'Missouri' programme was predicated on research showing that working with the family, rather than bypassing the parents, is the most effective way of helping children get off to the best possible start in life. The four-year pilot study included 380 families who were about to have their first child and who represented a cross-section of socio-economic status, age and family configurations. They included single-parent and two-parent families, families in which both parents worked, and families with either the mother or father at home.

The programme involved trained parent-educators visiting the parents' home and working with the parent, or parents, and the child. Information on child development, and guidance on things to look for and expect as the child grows were provided, plus guidance in fostering the child's intellectual, language, social and motor-skill development. Periodic check-ups of the child's educational and sensory development (hearing and vision) were made to detect possible handicaps that interfere with growth and development. Medical problems were referred to professionals.

Parent-educators made personal visits to homes and monthly group meetings were held with other new parents to share experience and discuss topics of interest. Parent resource centres, located in school buildings, offered learning materials for families and facilitators for child care.

E

At the age of three, the children who had been involved in the 'Missouri' programme were evaluated alongside a cross-section of children selected from the same range of socio-economic backgrounds and family situations, and also a random sample of children that age. The results were phenomenal. By the age of three, the children in the programme were significantly more advanced in language development than their peers, had made greater strides in problem solving and other intellectual skills, and were further along in social development. In fact, the average child on the programme was performing at the level of the top 15 to 20 per cent of their peers in such things as auditory comprehension, verbal ability and language ability.

Most important of all, the traditional measures of 'risk', such as parents' age and education, or whether they were a single parent, bore little or no relationship to the measures of achievement and language development. Children in the programme performed equally well regardless of socio-economic disadvantages. Child abuse was virtually eliminated. The one factor that was found to affect the child's development was family stress leading to a poor quality of parent–child interaction. That interaction was not necessarily bad in poorer families.

F

These research findings are exciting. There is growing evidence in New Zealand that children from poorer socio-economic backgrounds are arriving at school less well developed and that our school system tends to perpetuate that disadvantage. The initiative outlined above could break that cycle of disadvantage. The concept of working with parents in their homes, or at their place of work, contrasts quite markedly with the report of the Early Childhood Care and Education Working Group. Their focus is on getting children and mothers access to childcare and institutionalised early childhood education. Education from the age of three to five is undoubtedly vital, but without a similar focus on parent education and on the vital importance of the first three years, some evidence indicates that it will not be enough to overcome educational inequity.

Questions 1–4

Reading Passage 1 has six sections, **A–F**.

Which paragraph contains the following information?

Write the correct letter A–F in boxes 1–4 on your answer sheet.

1   details of the range of family types involved in an education programme

2   reasons why a child's early years are so important

3   reasons why an education programme failed

4   a description of the positive outcomes of an education programme

Questions 5–10

Classify the following features as characterising

> **A**   *the 'Headstart' programme*
> **B**   *the 'Missouri' programme*
> **C**   *both the 'Headstart' and the 'Missouri' programmes*
> **D**   *neither the 'Headstart' nor the 'Missouri' programme*

Write the correct letter A, B, C or D in boxes 5–10 on your answer sheet.

5   was administered to a variety of poor and wealthy families

6   continued with follow-up assistance in elementary schools

7   did not succeed in its aim

8   supplied many forms of support and training to parents

9   received insufficient funding

10   was designed to improve pre-schoolers' educational development

Questions 11–13

Do the following statements agree with the information given in Reading Passage 1?

In boxes 11–13 on your answer sheet, write

> **TRUE**   *if the statement agrees with the information*
> **FALSE**   *if the statement contradicts the information*
> **NOT GIVEN**   *if there is no information on this*

11   Most 'Missouri' programme three-year-olds scored highly in areas such as listening, speaking, reasoning and interacting with others.

12   'Missouri' programme children of young, uneducated, single parents scored less highly on the tests.

13   The richer families in the 'Missouri' programme had higher stress levels.

READING PASSAGE 2

*You should spend about 20 minutes on **Questions 14–26**, which are based on Reading Passage 2 on the following pages.*

Questions 14–17

Reading Passage 2 has six paragraphs, **A–F**.

*Choose the correct heading for paragraphs **B** and **D–F** from the list of headings below.*

*Write the correct number **i–viii** in boxes 14–17 on your answer sheet.*

```
┌─────────────────────────────────────────────────────────┐
│                    List of Headings                       │
│                                                           │
│   i      Effects of irrigation on sedimentation           │
│   ii     The danger of flooding the Cairo area            │
│   iii    Causing pollution in the Mediterranean           │
│   iv     Interrupting a natural process                   │
│   v      The threat to food production                    │
│   vi     Less valuable sediment than before               │
│   vii    Egypt's disappearing coastline                   │
│   viii   Looking at the long-term impact                  │
│                                                           │
└─────────────────────────────────────────────────────────┘
```

Example	Paragraph **A**	*Answer*	**vii**

14	Paragraph **B**

Example	Paragraph **C**	*Answer*	**vi**

15	Paragraph **D**

16	Paragraph **E**

17	Paragraph **F**

Disappearing Delta

A The fertile land of the Nile delta is being eroded along Egypt's Mediterranean coast at an astounding rate, in some parts estimated at 100 metres per year. In the past, land scoured away from the coastline by the currents of the Mediterranean Sea used to be replaced by sediment brought down to the delta by the River Nile, but this is no longer happening.

B Up to now, people have blamed this loss of delta land on the two large dams at Aswan in the south of Egypt, which hold back virtually all of the sediment that used to flow down the river. Before the dams were built, the Nile flowed freely, carrying huge quantities of sediment north from Africa's interior to be deposited on the Nile delta. This continued for 7,000 years, eventually covering a region of over 22,000 square kilometres with layers of fertile silt. Annual flooding brought in new, nutrient-rich soil to the delta region, replacing what had been washed away by the sea, and dispensing with the need for fertilizers in Egypt's richest food-growing area. But when the Aswan dams were constructed in the 20th century to provide electricity and irrigation, and to protect the huge population centre of Cairo and its surrounding areas from annual flooding and drought, most of the sediment with its natural fertilizer accumulated up above the dam in the southern, upstream half of Lake Nasser, instead of passing down to the delta.

C Now, however, there turns out to be more to the story. It appears that the sediment-free water emerging from the Aswan dams picks up silt and sand as it erodes the river bed and banks on the 800-kilometre trip to Cairo. Daniel Jean Stanley of the Smithsonian Institute noticed that water samples taken in Cairo, just before the river enters the delta, indicated that the river sometimes carries more than 850 grams of sediment per cubic metre of water – almost half of what it carried before the dams were built. 'I'm ashamed to say that the significance of this didn't strike me until after I had read 50 or 60 studies,' says Stanley in *Marine Geology*. 'There is still a lot of sediment coming into the delta, but virtually no sediment comes out into the Mediterranean to replenish the coastline. So this sediment must be trapped on the delta itself.'

D Once north of Cairo, most of the Nile water is diverted into more than 10,000 kilometres of irrigation canals and only a small proportion reaches the sea directly through the rivers in the delta. The water in the irrigation canals is still or very slow-moving and thus cannot carry sediment, Stanley explains. The sediment sinks to the bottom of the canals and then is added to fields by farmers or pumped with the water into the four large freshwater lagoons that are located near the outer edges of the delta. So very little of it actually reaches the coastline to replace what is being washed away by the Mediterranean currents.

E The farms on the delta plains and fishing and aquaculture in the lagoons account for much of Egypt's food supply. But by the time the sediment has come to rest in the fields and lagoons it is laden with municipal, industrial and agricultural waste from the Cairo region, which is home to more than 40 million people. 'Pollutants are building up faster and faster,' says Stanley.

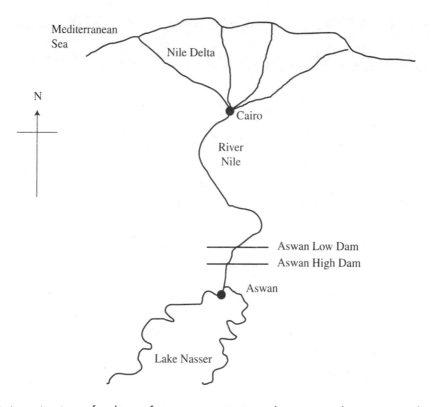

Based on his investigations of sediment from the delta lagoons, Frederic Siegel of George Washington University concurs. 'In Manzalah Lagoon, for example, the increase in mercury, lead, copper and zinc coincided with the building of the High Dam at Aswan, the availability of cheap electricity, and the development of major power-based industries,' he says. Since that time the concentration of mercury has increased significantly. Lead from engines that use leaded fuels and from other industrial sources has also increased dramatically. These poisons can easily enter the food chain, affecting the productivity of fishing and farming. Another problem is that agricultural wastes include fertilizers which stimulate increases in plant growth in the lagoons and upset the ecology of the area, with serious effects on the fishing industry.

F According to Siegel, international environmental organisations are beginning to pay closer attention to the region, partly because of the problems of erosion and pollution of the Nile delta, but principally because they fear the impact this situation could have on the whole Mediterranean coastal ecosystem. But there are no easy solutions. In the immediate future, Stanley believes that one solution would be to make artificial floods to flush out the delta waterways, in the same way that natural floods did before the construction of the dams. He says, however, that in the long term an alternative process such as desalination may have to be used to increase the amount of water available. 'In my view, Egypt must devise a way to have more water running through the river and the delta,' ·says Stanley. Easier said than done in a desert region with a rapidly growing population.

Questions 18–23

Do the following statements reflect the claims of the writer in Reading Passage 2?

In boxes 18–23 on your answer sheet, write

> **YES**   *if the statement reflects the claims of the writer*
> **NO**   *if the statement contradicts the claims of the writer*
> **NOT GIVEN**   *if it is impossible to say what the writer thinks about this*

18 Coastal erosion occurred along Egypt's Mediterranean coast before the building of the Aswan dams.

19 Some people predicted that the Aswan dams would cause land loss before they were built.

20 The Aswan dams were built to increase the fertility of the Nile delta.

21 Stanley found that the levels of sediment in the river water in Cairo were relatively high.

22 Sediment in the irrigation canals on the Nile delta causes flooding.

23 Water is pumped from the irrigation canals into the lagoons.

Questions 24–26

Complete the summary of paragraphs E and F with the list of words A–H below.

Write the correct letter A–H in boxes 24–26 on your answer sheet.

In addition to the problem of coastal erosion, there has been a marked increase in the level of **24** .... contained in the silt deposited in the Nile delta. To deal with this, Stanley suggests the use of **25** .... in the short term, and increasing the amount of water available through **26** .... in the longer term.

A artificial floods	**B** desalination	**C** delta waterways	**D** natural floods
E nutrients	**F** pollutants	**G** population control	**H** sediment

READING PASSAGE 3

*You should spend about 20 minutes on **Questions 27–40**, which are based on Reading Passage 3 below.*

The Return of Artificial Intelligence

It is becoming acceptable again to talk of computers performing human tasks such as problem-solving and pattern-recognition

A After years in the wilderness, the term 'artificial intelligence' (AI) seems poised to make a comeback. AI was big in the 1980s but vanished in the 1990s. It re-entered public consciousness with the release of *AI*, a movie about a robot boy. This has ignited public debate about AI, but the term is also being used once more within the computer industry. Researchers, executives and marketing people are now using the expression without irony or inverted commas. And it is not always hype. The term is being applied, with some justification, to products that depend on technology that was originally developed by AI researchers. Admittedly, the rehabilitation of the term has a long way to go, and some firms still prefer to avoid using it. But the fact that others are starting to use it again suggests that AI has moved on from being seen as an over-ambitious and under-achieving field of research.

B The field was launched, and the term 'artificial intelligence' coined, at a conference in 1956 by a group of researchers that included Marvin Minsky, John McCarthy, Herbert Simon and Alan Newell, all of whom went on to become leading figures in the field. The expression provided an attractive but informative name for a research programme that encompassed such previously disparate fields as operations research, cybernetics, logic and computer science. The goal they shared was an attempt to capture or mimic human abilities using machines. That said, different groups of researchers attacked different problems, from speech recognition to chess playing, in different ways; AI unified the field in name only. But it was a term that captured the public imagination.

C Most researchers agree that AI peaked around 1985. A public reared on science-fiction movies and excited by the growing power of computers had high expectations. For years, AI researchers had implied that a breakthrough was just around the corner. Marvin Minsky said in 1967 that within a generation the problem of creating 'artificial intelligence' would be substantially solved. Prototypes of medical-diagnosis programs and speech recognition software appeared to be making progress. It proved to be a false dawn. Thinking computers and household robots failed to materialise, and a backlash ensued. 'There was undue optimism in the early 1980s,' says David Leake, a researcher at Indiana University. 'Then when people realised these were hard problems, there was retrenchment. By the late 1980s, the term AI was being avoided by many researchers, who opted instead to align themselves with specific sub-disciplines such as neural networks, agent technology, case-based reasoning, and so on.'

D Ironically, in some ways AI was a victim of its own success. Whenever an apparently mundane problem was solved, such as building a system that could land an aircraft unattended, the problem was deemed not to have been AI in the first place. 'If it works, it can't be AI,' as Dr Leake characterises it. The effect of repeatedly moving the goal-posts in this way was that AI came to refer to 'blue-sky' research that was still years away from commercialisation. Researchers joked that AI stood for 'almost implemented'. Meanwhile, the technologies that made it onto the market, such as speech recognition, language translation and decision-support software, were no longer regarded as AI. Yet all three once fell well within the umbrella of AI research.

E But the tide may now be turning, according to Dr Leake. HNC Software of San Diego, backed by a government agency, reckon that their new approach to artificial intelligence is the most powerful and promising approach ever discovered. HNC claim that their system, based on a cluster of 30 processors, could be used to spot camouflaged vehicles on a battlefield or extract a voice signal from a noisy background – tasks humans can do well, but computers cannot. 'Whether or not their technology lives up to the claims made for it, the fact that HNC are emphasising the use of AI is itself an interesting development,' says Dr Leake.

F Another factor that may boost the prospects for AI in the near future is that investors are now looking for firms using clever technology, rather than just a clever business model, to differentiate themselves. In particular, the problem of information overload, exacerbated by the growth of e-mail and the explosion in the number of web pages, means there are plenty of opportunities for new technologies to help filter and categorise information – classic AI problems. That may mean that more artificial intelligence companies will start to emerge to meet this challenge.

G The 1969 film, *2001: A Space Odyssey*, featured an intelligent computer called HAL 9000. As well as understanding and speaking English, HAL could play chess and even learned to lipread. HAL thus encapsulated the optimism of the 1960s that intelligent computers would be widespread by 2001. But 2001 has been and gone, and there is still no sign of a HAL-like computer. Individual systems can play chess or transcribe speech, but a general theory of machine intelligence still remains elusive. It may be, however, that the comparison with HAL no longer seems quite so important, and AI can now be judged by what it can do, rather than by how well it matches up to a 30-year-old science-fiction film. 'People are beginning to realise that there are impressive things that these systems can do,' says Dr Leake hopefully.

Questions 27–31

Reading Passage 3 has seven paragraphs, A–G.

Which paragraph contains the following information?

Write the correct letter A–G in boxes 27–31 on your answer sheet.

NB You may use any letter more than once.

27   how AI might have a military impact

28   the fact that AI brings together a range of separate research areas

29   the reason why AI has become a common topic of conversation again

30   how AI could help deal with difficulties related to the amount of information available electronically

31   where the expression AI was first used

Questions 32–37

Do the following statements agree with the information given in Reading Passage 3?

In boxes 32–37 on your answer sheet, write

> **TRUE**   *if the statement agrees with the information*
> **FALSE**   *if the statement contradicts the information*
> **NOT GIVEN**   *if there is no information about this*

32   The researchers who launched the field of AI had worked together on other projects in the past.

33   In 1985, AI was at its lowest point.

34   Research into agent technology was more costly than research into neural networks.

35   Applications of AI have already had a degree of success.

36   The problems waiting to be solved by AI have not changed since 1967.

37   The film *2001: A Space Odyssey* reflected contemporary ideas about the potential of AI computers.

Questions 38–40

Choose the correct letter A, B, C or D.

Write your answers in boxes 38–40 on your answer sheet.

38 According to researchers, in the late 1980s there was a feeling that

    A   a general theory of AI would never be developed.
    B   original expectations of AI may not have been justified.
    C   a wide range of applications was close to fruition.
    D   more powerful computers were the key to further progress.

39 In Dr Leake's opinion, the reputation of AI suffered as a result of

    A   changing perceptions.
    B   premature implementation.
    C   poorly planned projects.
    D   commercial pressures.

40 The prospects for AI may benefit from

    A   existing AI applications.
    B   new business models.
    C   orders from internet-only companies.
    D   new investment priorities.

WRITING

WRITING TASK 1

You should spend about 20 minutes on this task.

> **The map below is of the town of Garlsdon. A new supermarket (S) is planned for the town. The map shows two possible sites for the supermarket.**
>
> **Summarise the information by selecting and reporting the main features, and make comparisons where relevant.**

Write at least 150 words.

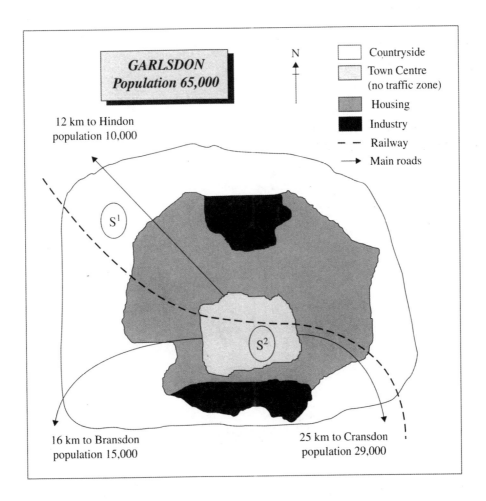

WRITING TASK 2

You should spend about 40 minutes on this task.

Write about the following topic:

> *Some people think that a sense of competition in children should be encouraged. Others believe that children who are taught to co-operate rather than compete become more useful adults.*
>
> *Discuss both these views and give your own opinion.*

Give reasons for your answer and include any relevant examples from your own knowledge or experience.

Write at least 250 words.

SPEAKING

PART 1

The examiner asks the candidate about him/herself, his/her home, work or studies and other familiar topics.

EXAMPLE

Entertainment

- Do you prefer relaxing at home or going out in the evening? [Why?]
- When you go out for an evening, what do you like to do?
- How popular is this with other people in your country?
- Is there any kind of entertainment you do not like? [Why/Why not?]

PART 2

Describe one of your friends.
 	
You should say:
    how you met
    how long you have known each other
    how you spend time together
and explain why you like this person.

You will have to talk about the topic for one to two minutes.
You have one minute to think about what you're going to say.
You can make some notes to help you if you wish.

PART 3

Discussion topics:

Qualities of friends

Example questions:
What do you think are the most important qualities for friends to have?
Which are more important to people, their family or their friends? Why?
What do you think causes friendships to break up?

Other relationships

Example questions:
What other types of relationship, apart from friends or family, are important in people's lives today?
Have relationships with neighbours where you live changed in recent years? How?
How important do you think it is for a person to spend some time alone? Why/Why not?

Test 4

SECTION 1   *Questions 1–10*

Questions 1–10

Complete the form below.

Write **NO MORE THAN THREE WORDS AND/OR NUMBERS** *for each answer.*

HOST FAMILY APPLICANT

Example	*Answer*
Name:	Jenny Chan

Present address: *Sea View Guest House*, **1** ....

Daytime phone number: *2237676*

      [NB Best time to contact is **2** .... *]*

Age: *19*

Intended length of stay: **3** ....

Occupation while in UK: *student*

General level of English: **4** ....

Preferred location: *in the* **5** ....

Special diet: **6** ....

Other requirements: *own facilities*

                 own television

                 7 ....

                 to be **8** ....

Maximum price: **9** £ .... *a week*

Preferred starting date: **10** ....

SECTION 2   *Questions 11–20*

Questions 11–13

Complete the sentences below.

*Write **NO MORE THAN TWO WORDS** for each answer.*

11   The next meeting of the soccer club will be in the .... in King's Park on 2 July.

12   The first event is a ....

13   At the final dinner, players receive ....

Questions 14–17

Complete the table below.

*Write **NO MORE THAN THREE WORDS AND/OR A NUMBER** for each answer.*

Competition	Number of Teams	Games Begin	Training Session (in King's Park)
Junior	**14**	8.30 am	**15** ....
Senior	**16**	2.00 pm	**17** ....

Questions 18–20

Complete the table below.

*Write **NO MORE THAN THREE WORDS** for each answer.*

Name of Office Bearer	Responsibility
Robert Young: President	to manage meetings
Gina Costello: Treasurer	to **18** ....
David West: Secretary	to **19** ....
Jason Dokic: Head Coach	to **20** ....

SECTION 3   *Questions 21–30*

Questions 21–24

Complete the notes below.

*Write **NO MORE THAN THREE WORDS** for each answer.*

Box Telecom

Problems: been affected by
- drop in 21 ....
- growing 22 ....
- delays due to a strike

Causes of problems:
- high 23 ....
- lack of good 24 ....

Questions 25–27

*Choose the correct letter, **A**, **B** or **C**.*

25 What does Karin think the company will do?

    A   look for private investors
    B   accept a takeover offer
    C   issue some new shares

26 How does the tutor suggest the company can recover?

    A   by appointing a new managing director
    B   by changing the way it is organised
    C   by closing some of its retail outlets

27 The tutor wants Jason and Karin to produce a report which

    A   offers solutions to Box Telecom's problems.
    B   analyses the UK market.
    C   compares different companies.

Questions 28–30

Which opinion does each person express about Box Telecom?

*Choose your answers from the box and write the letters **A–F** next to questions 28–30.*

A	its workers are motivated
B	it has too little investment
C	it will overcome its problems
D	its marketing campaign needs improvement
E	it is old-fashioned
F	it has strong managers

28 Karin ....

29 Jason ....

30 the tutor ....

SECTION 4   *Questions 31–40*

Questions 31–36

Choose the correct letter, A, B or C.

31 During the first week of term, students are invited to

   A be shown round the library by the librarian.
   B listen to descriptions of library resources.
   C do an intensive course in the computer centre.

32 The speaker warns the students that

   A internet materials can be unreliable.
   B downloaded information must be acknowledged.
   C computer access may be limited at times.

33 The library is acquiring more CDs as a resource because

   A they are a cheap source of information.
   B they take up very little space.
   C they are more up to date than the reference books.

34 Students are encouraged to use journals online because

   A the articles do not need to be returned to the shelves.
   B reading online is cheaper than photocopying articles.
   C the stock of printed articles is to be reduced.

35 Why might some students continue to use reference books?

   A they can be taken away from the library
   B they provide information unavailable elsewhere
   C they can be borrowed for an extended loan period

36 What is the responsibility of the Training Supervisor?

   A to supervise and support library staff
   B to provide orientation to the library facilities
   C to identify needs and inform section managers

Questions 37–40

Which section of the university will help postgraduate students with their dissertations in the following ways?

A   the postgraduate's own department or tutor
B   library staff
C   another section of the university

Write the correct letter, A, B or C, next to questions 37–40.

37   training in specialised computer programs   ....

38   advising on bibliography presentation   ....

39   checking the draft of the dissertation   ....

40   providing language support   ....

READING

READING PASSAGE 1

*You should spend about 20 minutes on **Questions 1–13**, which are based on Reading Passage 1 on the following pages.*

Questions 1–3

Reading Passage 1 has three sections, **A–C**.

Choose the correct heading for each section from the list of headings below.

*Write the correct number **i–vi** in boxes 1–3 on your answer sheet.*

	List of Headings
i	The expansion of international tourism in recent years
ii	How local communities can balance their own needs with the demands of wilderness tourism
iii	Fragile regions and the reasons for the expansion of tourism there
iv	Traditional methods of food-supply in fragile regions
v	Some of the disruptive effects of wilderness tourism
vi	The economic benefits of mass tourism

1   Section **A**

2   Section **B**

3   Section **C**

The Impact of Wilderness Tourism

A

The market for tourism in remote areas is booming as never before. Countries all across the world are actively promoting their 'wilderness' regions – such as mountains, Arctic lands, deserts, small islands and wetlands – to high-spending tourists. The attraction of these areas is obvious: by definition, wilderness tourism requires little or no initial investment. But that does not mean that there is no cost. As the 1992 United Nations Conference on Environment and Development recognized, these regions are fragile (i.e. highly vulnerable to abnormal pressures) not just in terms of their ecology, but also in terms of the culture of their inhabitants. The three most significant types of fragile environment in these respects, and also in terms of the proportion of the Earth's surface they cover, are deserts, mountains and Arctic areas. An important characteristic is their marked seasonality, with harsh conditions prevailing for many months each year. Consequently, most human activities, including tourism, are limited to quite clearly defined parts of the year.

Tourists are drawn to these regions by their natural landscape beauty and the unique cultures of their indigenous people. And poor governments in these isolated areas have welcomed the new breed of 'adventure tourist', grateful for the hard currency they bring. For several years now, tourism has been the prime source of foreign exchange in Nepal and Bhutan. Tourism is also a key element in the economies of Arctic zones such as Lapland and Alaska and in desert areas such as Ayers Rock in Australia and Arizona's Monument Valley.

B

Once a location is established as a main tourist destination, the effects on the local community are profound. When hill-farmers, for example, can make more money in a few weeks working as porters for foreign trekkers than they can in a year working in their fields, it is not surprising that many of them give up their farm-work, which is thus left to other members of the family. In some hill-regions, this has led to a serious decline in farm output and a change in the local diet, because there is insufficient labour to maintain terraces and irrigation systems and tend to crops. The result has been that many people in these regions have turned to outside supplies of rice and other foods.

In Arctic and desert societies, year-round survival has traditionally depended on hunting animals and fish and collecting fruit over a relatively short season. However, as some inhabitants become involved in tourism, they no longer have time to collect wild food; this has led to increasing dependence on bought food and stores. Tourism is not always the culprit behind such changes. All kinds of wage labour, or government handouts, tend to undermine traditional survival systems. Whatever the cause, the dilemma is always the same: what happens if these new, external sources of income dry up?

The physical impact of visitors is another serious problem associated with the growth in adventure tourism. Much attention has focused on erosion along major trails, but perhaps more important are the deforestation and impacts on water supplies arising from the need to provide tourists with cooked food and hot showers. In both mountains and deserts, slow-growing trees are often the main sources of fuel and water supplies may be limited or vulnerable to degradation through heavy use.

C

Stories about the problems of tourism have become legion in the last few years. Yet it does not have to be a problem. Although tourism inevitably affects the region in which it takes place, the costs to these fragile environments and their local cultures can be minimized. Indeed, it can even be a vehicle for reinvigorating local cultures, as has happened with the Sherpas of Nepal's Khumbu Valley and in some Alpine villages. And a growing number of adventure tourism operators are trying to ensure that their activities benefit the local population and environment over the long term.

In the Swiss Alps, communities have decided that their future depends on integrating tourism more effectively with the local economy. Local concern about the rising number of second home developments in the Swiss Pays d'Enhaut resulted in limits being imposed on their growth. There has also been a renaissance in communal cheese production in the area, providing the locals with a reliable source of income that does not depend on outside visitors.

Many of the Arctic tourist destinations have been exploited by outside companies, who employ transient workers and repatriate most of the profits to their home base. But some Arctic communities are now operating tour businesses themselves, thereby ensuring that the benefits accrue locally. For instance, a native corporation in Alaska, employing local people, is running an air tour from Anchorage to Kotzebue, where tourists eat Arctic food, walk on the tundra and watch local musicians and dancers.

Native people in the desert regions of the American Southwest have followed similar strategies, encouraging tourists to visit their pueblos and reservations to purchase high-quality handicrafts and artwork. The Acoma and San Ildefonso pueblos have established highly profitable pottery businesses, while the Navajo and Hopi groups have been similarly successful with jewellery.

Too many people living in fragile environments have lost control over their economies, their culture and their environment when tourism has penetrated their homelands. Merely restricting tourism cannot be the solution to the imbalance, because people's desire to see new places will not just disappear. Instead, communities in fragile environments must achieve greater control over tourism ventures in their regions, in order to balance their needs and aspirations with the demands of tourism. A growing number of communities are demonstrating that, with firm communal decision-making, this is possible. The critical question now is whether this can become the norm, rather than the exception.

Questions 4–9

Do the following statements reflect the opinion of the writer of Reading Passage 1?

In boxes 4–9 on your answer sheet, write

> **YES**   *if the statement reflects the opinion of the writer*
> **NO**   *if the statement contradicts the opinion of the writer*
> **NOT GIVEN** *if it is impossible to say what the writer thinks about this*

4   The low financial cost of setting up wilderness tourism makes it attractive to many countries.

5   Deserts, mountains and Arctic regions are examples of environments that are both ecologically and culturally fragile.

6   Wilderness tourism operates throughout the year in fragile areas.

7   The spread of tourism in certain hill-regions has resulted in a fall in the amount of food produced locally.

8   Traditional food-gathering in desert societies was distributed evenly over the year.

9   Government handouts do more damage than tourism does to traditional patterns of food-gathering.

Questions 10–13

Complete the table below.

*Choose **ONE WORD** from Reading Passage 1 for each answer.*

Write your answers in boxes 10–13 on your answer sheet.

The positive ways in which some local communities have responded to tourism	
People/Location	**Activity**
Swiss Pays d'Enhaut	Revived production of **10** ....
Arctic communities	Operate **11** .... businesses
Acoma and San Ildefonso	Produce and sell **12** ....
Navajo and Hopi	Produce and sell **13** ....

READING PASSAGE 2

*You should spend about 20 minutes on **Questions 14–26**, which are based on Reading Passage 2 below.*

Flawed Beauty: the problem with toughened glass

On 2nd August 1999, a particularly hot day in the town of Cirencester in the UK, a large pane of toughened glass in the roof of a shopping centre at Bishops Walk shattered without warning and fell from its frame. When fragments were analysed by experts at the giant glass manufacturer Pilkington, which had made the pane, they found that minute crystals of nickel sulphide trapped inside the glass had almost certainly caused the failure.

'The glass industry is aware of the issue,' says Brian Waldron, chairman of the standards committee at the Glass and Glazing Federation, a British trade association, and standards development officer at Pilkington. But he insists that cases are few and far between. 'It's a very rare phenomenon,' he says.

Others disagree. 'On average I see about one or two buildings a month suffering from nickel sulphide related failures,' says Barrie Josie, a consultant engineer involved in the Bishops Walk investigation. Other experts tell of similar experiences. Tony Wilmott of London-based consulting engineers Sandberg, and Simon Armstrong at CladTech Associates in Hampshire both say they know of hundreds of cases. 'What you hear is only the tip of the iceberg,' says Trevor Ford, a glass expert at Resolve Engineering in Brisbane, Queensland. He believes the reason is simple: 'No-one wants bad press.'

Toughened glass is found everywhere, from cars and bus shelters to the windows, walls and roofs of thousands of buildings around the world. It's easy to see why. This glass has five times the strength of standard glass, and when it does break it shatters into tiny cubes rather than large, razor-sharp shards. Architects love it because large panels can be bolted together to make transparent walls, and turning it into ceilings and floors is almost as easy.

It is made by heating a sheet of ordinary glass to about 620°C to soften it slightly, allowing its structure to expand, and then cooling it rapidly with jets of cold air. This causes the outer layer of the pane to contract and solidify before the interior. When the interior finally solidifies and shrinks, it exerts a pull on the outer layer that leaves it in permanent compression and produces a tensile force inside the glass. As cracks propagate best in materials under tension, the compressive force on the surface must be overcome before the pane will break, making it more resistant to cracking.

The problem starts when glass contains nickel sulphide impurities. Trace amounts of nickel and sulphur are usually present in the raw materials used to make glass, and nickel can also be introduced by fragments of nickel alloys falling into the molten glass. As the glass is heated, these atoms react to form tiny crystals of nickel sulphide. Just a tenth of a gram of nickel in the furnace can create up to 50,000 crystals.

These crystals can exist in two forms: a dense form called the alpha phase, which is stable at high temperatures, and a less dense form called the beta phase, which is stable at room temperatures. The high temperatures used in the toughening process convert all the crystals to the dense, compact alpha form. But the subsequent cooling is so rapid that the crystals don't have time to change back to the beta phase. This leaves unstable alpha crystals in the glass, primed like a coiled spring, ready to revert to the beta phase without warning.

When this happens, the crystals expand by up to 4%. And if they are within the central, tensile region of the pane, the stresses this unleashes can shatter the whole sheet. The time that elapses before failure occurs is unpredictable. It could happen just months after manufacture, or decades later, although if the glass is heated – by sunlight, for example – the process is speeded up. Ironically, says Graham Dodd, of consulting engineers Arup in London, the oldest pane of toughened glass known to have failed due to nickel sulphide inclusions was in Pilkington's glass research building in Lathom, Lancashire. The pane was 27 years old.

Data showing the scale of the nickel sulphide problem is almost impossible to find. The picture is made more complicated by the fact that these crystals occur in batches. So even if, on average, there is only one inclusion in 7 tonnes of glass, if you experience one nickel sulphide failure in your building, that probably means you've got a problem in more than one pane. Josie says that in the last decade he has worked on over 15 buildings with the number of failures into double figures.

One of the worst examples of this is Waterfront Place, which was completed in 1990. Over the following decade the 40-storey Brisbane block suffered a rash of failures. Eighty panes of its toughened glass shattered due to inclusions before experts were finally called in. John Barry, an expert in nickel sulphide contamination at the University of Queensland, analysed every glass pane in the building. Using a studio camera, a photographer went up in a cradle to take photos of every pane. These were scanned under a modified microfiche reader for signs of nickel sulphide crystals. 'We discovered at least another 120 panes with potentially dangerous inclusions which were then replaced,' says Barry. 'It was a very expensive and time-consuming process that took around six months to complete.' Though the project cost A$1.6 million (nearly £700,000), the alternative – re-cladding the entire building – would have cost ten times as much.

Questions 14–17

Look at the following people and the list of statements below.

Match each person with the correct statement.

Write the correct letter A–H in boxes 14–17 on your answer sheet.

14   Brian Waldron

15   Trevor Ford

16   Graham Dodd

17   John Barry

List of Statements

A   suggests that publicity about nickel sulphide failure has been suppressed

B   regularly sees cases of nickel sulphide failure

C   closely examined all the glass in one building

D   was involved with the construction of Bishops Walk

E   recommended the rebuilding of Waterfront Place

F   thinks the benefits of toughened glass are exaggerated

G   claims that nickel sulphide failure is very unusual

H   refers to the most extreme case of delayed failure

Questions 18–23

Complete the summary with the list of words A–P below.

Write your answers in boxes 18–23 on your answer sheet.

Toughened Glass

Toughened glass is favoured by architects because it is much stronger than ordinary glass, and the fragments are not as **18** .... when it breaks. However, it has one disadvantage: it can shatter **19** .... This fault is a result of the manufacturing process. Ordinary glass is first heated, then cooled very **20** .... The outer layer **21** .... before the inner layer, and the tension between the two layers which is created because of this makes the glass stronger. However, if the glass contains nickel sulphide impurities, crystals of nickel sulphide are formed. These are unstable, and can expand suddenly, particularly if the weather is **22** .... If this happens, the pane of glass may break. The frequency with which such problems occur is **23** .... by glass experts. Furthermore, the crystals cannot be detected without sophisticated equipment.

A numerous	**B** detected	**C** quickly
D agreed	**E** warm	**F** sharp
G expands	**H** slowly	**I** unexpectedly
J removed	**K** contracts	**L** disputed
M cold	**N** moved	**O** small
P calculated		

Questions 24–26

Do the following statements agree with the information given in Reading Passage 2?

In boxes 24–26 on your answer sheet, write

TRUE   *if the statement agrees with the information*
FALSE   *if the statement contradicts the information*
NOT GIVEN   *if there is no information on this*

24   Little doubt was expressed about the reason for the Bishops Walk accident.

25   Toughened glass has the same appearance as ordinary glass.

26   There is plenty of documented evidence available about the incidence of nickel sulphide failure.

READING PASSAGE 3

*You should spend about 20 minutes on **Questions 27–40**, which are based on Reading Passage 3 below.*

The effects of light on plant and animal species

Light is important to organisms for two different reasons. Firstly it is used as a cue for the timing of daily and seasonal rhythms in both plants and animals, and secondly it is used to assist growth in plants.

Breeding in most organisms occurs during a part of the year only, and so a reliable cue is needed to trigger breeding behaviour. Day length is an excellent cue, because it provides a perfectly predictable pattern of change within the year. In the temperate zone in spring, temperatures fluctuate greatly from day to day, but day length increases steadily by a predictable amount. The seasonal impact of day length on physiological responses is called *photoperiodism*, and the amount of experimental evidence for this phenomenon is considerable. For example, some species of birds' breeding can be induced even in midwinter simply by increasing day length artificially (Wolfson 1964). Other examples of photoperiodism occur in plants. A *short-day plant* flowers when the day is less than a certain critical length. A *long-day plant* flowers after a certain critical day length is exceeded. In both cases the critical day length differs from species to species. Plants which flower after a period of vegetative growth, regardless of photoperiod, are known as *day-neutral plants*.

Breeding seasons in animals such as birds have evolved to occupy the part of the year in which offspring have the greatest chances of survival. Before the breeding season begins, food reserves must be built up to support the energy cost of reproduction, and to provide for young birds both when they are in the nest and after fledging. Thus many temperate-zone birds use the increasing day lengths in spring as a cue to begin the nesting cycle, because this is a point when adequate food resources will be assured.

The adaptive significance of photoperiodism in plants is also clear. Short-day plants that flower in spring in the temperate zone are adapted to maximising seedling growth during the growing season. Long-day plants are adapted for situations that require fertilization by insects, or a long period of seed ripening. Short-day plants that flower in the autumn in the temperate zone are able to build up food reserves over the growing season and over winter as seeds. Day-neutral plants have an evolutionary advantage when the connection between the favourable period for reproduction and day length is much less certain. For example, desert annuals germinate, flower and seed whenever suitable rainfall occurs, regardless of the day length.

The breeding season of some plants can be delayed to extraordinary lengths. Bamboos are perennial grasses that remain in a vegetative state for many years and then suddenly flower, fruit and die (Evans 1976). Every bamboo of the species *Chusquea abietifolia* on the island of Jamaica flowered, set seed and died during 1884. The next generation of bamboo flowered and died between 1916 and 1918, which suggests a vegetative cycle of about 31 years. The climatic trigger for this flowering cycle is not yet known, but the adaptive significance is clear. The simultaneous production of masses of bamboo seeds (in some cases lying 12 to 15 centimetres deep on the ground) is more than all the seed-eating animals can cope with at the time, so that some seeds escape being eaten and grow up to form the next generation (Evans 1976).

The second reason light is important to organisms is that it is essential for *photosynthesis*. This is the process by which plants use energy from the sun to convert carbon from soil or water into organic material for growth. The rate of photosynthesis in a plant can be measured by calculating the rate of its uptake of carbon. There is a wide range of photosynthetic responses of plants to variations in light intensity. Some plants reach maximal photosynthesis at one-quarter full sunlight, and others, like sugarcane, never reach a maximum, but continue to increase photosynthesis rate as light intensity rises.

Plants in general can be divided into two groups: *shade-tolerant* species and *shade-intolerant* species. This classification is commonly used in forestry and horticulture. Shade-tolerant plants have lower photosynthetic rates and hence have lower growth rates than those of shade-intolerant species. Plant species become adapted to living in a certain kind of habitat, and in the process evolve a series of characteristics that prevent them from occupying other habitats. Grime (1966) suggests that light may be one of the major components directing these adaptations. For example, eastern hemlock seedlings are shade-tolerant. They can survive in the forest understorey under very low light levels because they have a low photosynthetic rate.

Questions 27–33

Do the following statements agree with the information given in Reading Passage 3?

In boxes 27–33 on your answer sheet, write

>   **TRUE**   *if the statement agrees with the information*
>   **FALSE**   *if the statement contradicts the information*
>   **NOT GIVEN**   *if there is no information on this*

27   There is plenty of scientific evidence to support photoperiodism.

28   Some types of bird can be encouraged to breed out of season.

29   Photoperiodism is restricted to certain geographic areas.

30   Desert annuals are examples of long-day plants.

31   Bamboos flower several times during their life cycle.

32   Scientists have yet to determine the cue for *Chusquea abietifolia*'s seasonal rhythm.

33   Eastern hemlock is a fast-growing plant.

Questions 34–40

Complete the sentences.

*Choose **NO MORE THAN THREE WORDS** from the passage for each answer.*

Write your answers in boxes 34–40 on your answer sheet.

34   Day length is a useful cue for breeding in areas where .... are unpredictable.

35   Plants which do not respond to light levels are referred to as ....

36   Birds in temperate climates associate longer days with nesting and the availability of ....

37   Plants that flower when days are long often depend on .... to help them reproduce.

38   Desert annuals respond to .... as a signal for reproduction.

39   There is no limit to the photosynthetic rate in plants such as ....

40   Tolerance to shade is one criterion for the .... of plants in forestry and horticulture.

WRITING

WRITING TASK 1

You should spend about 20 minutes on this task.

> *The table below gives information about the underground railway systems in six cities.*
>
> *Summarise the information by selecting and reporting the main features, and make comparisons where relevant.*

Write at least 150 words.

Underground Railway Systems

City	Date opened	Kilometres of route	Passengers per year (in millions)
London	1863	394	775
Paris	1900	199	1191
Tokyo	1927	155	1927
Washington DC	1976	126	144
Kyoto	1981	11	45
Los Angeles	2001	28	50

WRITING TASK 2

You should spend about 40 minutes on this task.

Write about the following topic:

> *Research indicates that the characteristics we are born with have much more influence on our personality and development than any experiences we may have in our life.*
>
> *Which do you consider to be the major influence?*

Give reasons for your answer and include any relevant examples from your own knowledge or experience.

Write at least 250 words.

SPEAKING

PART 1

The examiner asks the candidate about him/herself, his/her home, work or studies and other familiar topics.

EXAMPLE

Clothes

- How important are clothes and fashion to you? [Why/Why not?]
- What kind of clothes do you dislike? [Why?]
- How different are the clothes you wear now from those you wore 10 years ago?
- What do you think the clothes we wear say about us?

PART 2

Describe a festival that is important in your country.

You should say:
  when the festival occurs
  what you did during it
  what you like or dislike about it
and explain why this festival is important.

You will have to talk about the topic for one to two minutes.
You have one minute to think about what you're going to say.
You can make some notes to help you if you wish.

PART 3

Discussion topics:

Purpose of festivals and celebrations

Example questions:
Why do you think festivals are important events in the working year?
Would you agree that the original significance of festivals is often lost today? Is it good or bad, do you think?
Do you think that new festivals will be introduced in the future? What kind?

Festivals and the media

Example questions:
What role does the media play in festivals, do you think?
Do you think it's good or bad to watch festivals on TV? Why?
How may globalisation affect different festivals around the world?

General Training: Reading and Writing Test A

SECTION 1   Questions 1–14

Read the information below and answer Questions 1–7.

MAIL ORDER BROCHURE

Want some great clothing ideas for your family?

Our key for clothing specials in July:

M for men   **W** for women   **C** for children

For under $10

Cotton socks **C**	– made of pure cotton for long wearing
Woollen socks **C**	– to keep young feet warm in winter
Sports socks **M**	– to go with jeans and other casual clothes
Patterned belts **W**	– to go with jeans and other casual clothes

For under $25

Cotton shirts **W**	– for day and evening wear
Silk shirts **M**	– five sizes, in designer colours, for that special social occasion
T-shirts **C**	– hard-wearing, white with a variety of animal motifs
Colour T-shirts **M W**	– cotton and polyester blend, plain colours, no ironing

For under $50

Blue jeans **M W**	– non-shrink, colourfast, small sizes only
Silk shirts **M W**	– plain and patterned, all sizes
Hooded jacket **C**	– protects from the wind, 4 sizes, large strong pockets
Jacket **W**	– waterproof with zipper front, all sizes

- Or you can buy a gift voucher so that someone else can choose. These come in $10, $20 and $50 amounts.

Additional monthly specials for July to September

July	– $10 voucher with any purchase over $60
August	– Travel alarm clock worth $19.95 free with purchases of $80 or more!
September	– Children's backpacks. Free with any credit card purchase over $75!

Note: Postage and packing charges

These are applied to each order as follows:

Within Australia:

$7.95 per address, regular post

$17.95 for Express Delivery Service (overnight)

Overseas:

Surface Mail (allow a minimum of two months for delivery)

Airmail (allow around two weeks delivery to most destinations)

Questions 1–7

Do the following statements agree with the information given in the text on the previous page?

In boxes 1–7 on your answer sheet, write

TRUE   *if the statement agrees with the information*
FALSE   *if the statement contradicts the information*
NOT GIVEN *if there is no information on this*

1   Women's cotton socks cost less than men's.

2   Men's silk shirts are available in more than five colours.

3   Children's T-shirts come in a variety of colours.

4   The child's jacket has four pockets.

5   If you buy clothes worth $80 in August, you will receive a free alarm clock.

6   The charge for special next-day delivery in Australia is $7.95.

7   All clothing is guaranteed to arrive within two months.

Questions 8–14

The list of 'New Book Releases' on the following page has nine book descriptions **A–I**.

Choose the correct title for each book from the list of book titles below.

*Write the correct number **i–xi** in boxes 8–14 on your answer sheet.*

List of Book Titles

i	Field Guide to Native Birds of Australia
ii	The Bush on Two Wheels: 100 Top Rides
iii	Bush Foods of Australian Aborigines
iv	A Pictorial History of the Dinosaur in Australia
v	Bushwalking in Australia
vi	World Geographica
vii	Driving Adventures for 4-wheel-drive Vehicles
viii	Survival Techniques in the Wild
ix	Encyclopaedia of Australian Wildlife
x	Guide to the Art of the Australian Desert
xi	Field Guide to Animals of the World

---

8   Book **A**

9   Book **B**

10   Book **C**

Example		*Answer*
	Book **D**	**vi**

11   Book **E**

12   Book **F**

13   Book **G**

14   Book **H**

Example	
	Book **I**

New Book Releases

A This book describes the creativity of Aboriginal people living in the driest parts of Australia. Stunning reproductions of paintings, beautiful photography and informative text.

B Pocket-sized maps and illustrations with detailed information on the nesting sites and migration patterns of Australia. This is a classic booklet suitable for both beginner and expert.

C Packed full of information for the avid hiker, this book is a must. Photographs, maps and practical advice will guide your journeys on foot through the forests of the southern continent.

D More than an atlas – this book contains maps, photographs and an abundance of information on the land and climate of countries from around the globe.

E Australia's premier mountain biking guidebook – taking you through a host of national parks and state forests.

F Here's the A–Z of Australian native animals – take an in-depth look at their lives and characteristics, through fantastic photographs and informative text.

G Graphic artists have worked with researchers and scientists to illustrate how these prehistoric animals lived and died on the Australian continent.

H A definitive handbook on outdoor safety – with a specific focus on equipment, nutrition, first aid, special clothing and bush skills.

I Detailed guides to 15 scenic car tours that will take you onto fascinating wilderness tracks and along routes that you could otherwise have missed.

SECTION 2   *Questions 15–27*

Read the advertisement below and answer Questions 15–20.

WORK & TRAVEL USA

Do you want to have the best summer holiday ever? Have you just graduated and want to escape for a unique experience abroad?

Only $1950 will make it all happen!

This unbeatable program fee includes:
- return flight from Sydney to Los Angeles (onward travel in USA not included)
- 3 months' insurance cover
- 2 nights' accommodation on arrival plus meet and greet and airport transfer
- arrival orientation by experienced **InterExchange** staff
- visa application fees

You also have:
- access to a J1 visa enabling you to work in the USA
- an extensive directory of employers
- **InterExchange** support throughout the program
- 24-hour emergency support throughout the length of the program

Call toll-free 1800 678 738

InterExchange has 50 years' experience in international student exchange programs. 18,000 students from around the world travel yearly to the USA on this very program. InterExchange can also offer you work opportunities in other countries.

WHAT IS INTEREXCHANGE?

InterExchange, one of the world's leading operators of international exchange programs and related services:
- is a non-profit, non-governmental organisation
- has 700 professional staff in 30 countries worldwide
- was founded in 1947

InterExchange operates these programs for students all around the world. It offers you trained and travelled staff, plus full support during the application process. You can choose any job that interests you anywhere in the USA, whether that is working in a law firm in Boston, a famous ski resort in Colorado or serving coffee and doughnuts in the buzzing streets of New York. You can select the period you work and the period you travel; you may want to work for 1 month and travel for 3, or work the entire duration of your stay. The choice is yours.

YOU CAN TAKE UP THIS OPPORTUNITY IF YOU ARE:
- a full-time student at an Australian university or TAFE college
- presently enrolled, or finishing this year, or you have deferred a year of study
- over 18 years old by November in the academic year in which you apply to **InterExchange**
- enthusiastic about the experience of a lifetime . . .

Sign up now!!

Questions 15–20

Do the following statements agree with the information given in the advertisement on the previous page?

In boxes 15–20 on your answer sheet, write

> **TRUE**   *if the statement agrees with the information*
> **FALSE**   *if the statement contradicts the information*
> **NOT GIVEN**   *if there is no information on this*

15 The program cost includes internal flights within the USA.

16 Emergency assistance offered in the program includes legal advice.

17 InterExchange offers similar programs in countries other than the USA.

18 InterExchange is part of a government program.

19 There are no restrictions on the type of job you can do.

20 There is an upper age limit for applicants.

Read the information below and answer Questions 21–27.

NETSCAPE　　　　　　　　　　　　　　　　　　　■ ■ ■

File Edit View Go Communicator Help

CONTENTS: ARTHUR PHILLIP COLLEGE

A	about Arthur Phillip College	**G**	learning methods
B	entry requirements	**H**	course fees
C	orientation for new students	**I**	study commitment
D	academic counselling service	**J**	assessment and results
E	credit courses to university	**K**	social activities and clubs
F	assistance for international students	**L**	what's new

Questions 21–27

Each of the short paragraphs below (**21–27**) gives information about Arthur Phillip College.

Read each paragraph and choose which of the linked sections of the website, A–L, would contain this information.

Write the correct letter A–L in boxes 21–27 on your answer sheet.

21   All students receive a transcript of results and relevant award documentation when they end their studies with the College.

22   On enrolment, all students receive automatic membership to the Social Club and Public Speaking Club. Students may choose to participate in any arranged activities. The College encourages and promotes interaction between students and teaching and non-teaching staff.

23   Successful completion and the achievement of an A or B result in some courses will enable students to achieve advanced standing in these subjects if they proceed to university study. For a list of the courses acceptable to a particular university, e-mail us your request with the name of the university and the course you are interested in.

24   Arthur Phillip College is one of the top business colleges in Sydney, Australia. The College offers a wide range of educational and training programs in business and related areas. Its accredited vocational training courses are designed to meet the needs of individual students and industry.

25   At Arthur Phillip College you will learn from lectures, seminars, case studies, group projects, individual assignments and class workshops. Lectures and seminars present concepts and ideas and provide for question-and-answer sessions. Students are expected to take an active role in the learning process through class participation, presentations and projects.

26   Courses at Arthur Phillip College involve an average of 25 hours per week of tuition time, with supervised group study accounting for a further 5 hours per week. At least 10 hours per week of individual study is also recommended for most courses.

27   During this program you will meet the Director of Studies, teachers and key administrative staff such as the Accommodation Officer and Student Counsellor so that, right from your first day, you will know how each of them can help you during your time at the College.

SECTION 3   *Questions 28–40*

Read the passage below and answer Questions 28–40.

LACK OF SLEEP

Section A

It is estimated that the average man or woman needs between seven-and-a-half and eight hours' sleep a night. Some can manage on a lot less. Baroness Thatcher, for example, was reported to be able to get by on four hours' sleep a night when she was Prime Minister of Britain. Dr Jill Wilkinson, senior lecturer in psychology at Surrey University and co-author of 'Psychology in Counselling and Therapeutic Practice', states that healthy individuals sleeping less than five hours or even as little as two hours in every 24 hours are rare, but represent a sizeable minority.

Section B

The latest beliefs are that the main purposes of sleep are to enable the body to rest and replenish, allowing time for repairs to take place and for tissue to be regenerated. One supporting piece of evidence for this rest-and-repair theory is that production of the growth hormone somatotropin, which helps tissue to regenerate, peaks while we are asleep. Lack of sleep, however, can compromise the immune system, muddle thinking, cause depression, promote anxiety and encourage irritability.

Section C

Researchers in San Diego deprived a group of men of sleep between 3am and 7am on just one night, and found that levels of their bodies' natural defences against viral infections had fallen significantly when measured the following morning. 'Sleep is essential for our physical and emotional well-being and there are few aspects of daily living that are not disrupted by the lack of it', says Professor William Regelson of Virginia University, a specialist in insomnia. 'Because it can seriously undermine the functioning of the immune system, sufferers are vulnerable to infection.'

Section D

For many people, lack of sleep is rarely a matter of choice. Some have problems getting to sleep, others with staying asleep until the morning. Despite popular belief that sleep is one long event, research shows that, in an average night, there are five stages of sleep and four cycles, during which the sequence of stages is repeated. In the first light phase, the heart rate and blood pressure go down and the muscles relax. In the next two stages, sleep gets progressively deeper. In stage four, usually reached after an hour, the slumber is so deep that, if awoken, the sleeper would be confused and disorientated. It is in this phase that sleep-walking can occur, with an average episode lasting no more than 15 minutes. In the fifth stage, the rapid eye movement (REM) stage, the heartbeat quickly gets back to normal levels, brain activity accelerates to daytime heights and above and the eyes move constantly beneath closed lids as if the sleeper is looking at something. During this stage, the body is almost paralysed. This REM phase is also the time when we dream.

Section E

Sleeping patterns change with age, which is why many people over 60 develop insomnia. In America, that age group consumes almost half the sleep medication on the market. One theory for the age-related change is that it is due to hormonal changes. The temperature rise occurs at daybreak in the young, but at three or four in the morning in the elderly. Age aside, it is estimated that roughly one in three people suffer some kind of sleep disturbance. Causes can be anything from pregnancy and stress to alcohol and heart disease. Smoking is a known handicap to sleep, with one survey showing that ex-smokers got to sleep in 18 minutes rather than their earlier average of 52 minutes.

Section F

Apart from self-help therapy such as regular exercise, there are psychological treatments, including relaxation training and therapy aimed at getting rid of pre-sleep worries and anxieties. There is also sleep reduction therapy, where the aim is to improve sleep quality by strictly regulating the time people go to bed and when they get up. Medication is regarded by many as a last resort and often takes the form of sleeping pills, normally benzodiazepines, which are minor tranquillisers.

Section G

Professor Regelson advocates the use of melatonin for treating sleep disorders. Melatonin is a naturally secreted hormone, located in the pineal gland deep inside the brain. The main function of the hormone is to control the body's biological clock, so we know when to sleep and when to wake. The gland detects light reaching it through the eye; when there is no light, it secretes the melatonin into the bloodstream, lowering the body temperature and helping to induce sleep. Melatonin pills contain a synthetic version of the hormone and are commonly used for jet lag as well as for sleep disturbance. John Nicholls, sales manager of one of America's largest health food shops, claims that sales of the pill have increased dramatically. He explains that it is sold in capsules, tablets, lozenges and mixed with herbs. It is not effective for all insomniacs, but many users have weaned themselves off sleeping tablets as a result of its application.

Questions 28–35

The passage on the previous pages has seven sections labelled **A–G**.

Which section contains the following information?

Write the correct letter A–G in boxes 28–35 on your answer sheet.

NB *You may use any letter more than once.*

28   the different amounts of sleep that people require

29   an investigation into the results of sleep deprivation

30   some reasons why people may suffer from sleep disorders

31   lifestyle changes which can help overcome sleep-related problems

32   a process by which sleep helps us to remain mentally and physically healthy

33   claims about a commercialised man-made product for sleeplessness

34   the role of physical changes in sleeping habits

35   the processes involved during sleep

Questions 36–40

Do the following statements agree with the information given in the passage?

In boxes 36–40 on your answer sheet, write

> **TRUE**   *if the statement agrees with the information*
> **FALSE**   *if the statement contradicts the information*
> **NOT GIVEN**   *if there is no information on this*

36   Sleep can cure some illnesses.

37   The various stages of sleep occur more than once a night.

38   Dreaming and sleep-walking occur at similar stages of sleep.

39   Sleepers move around a lot during the REM stage of sleep.

40   The body temperature rises relatively early in elderly people.

WRITING

WRITING TASK 1

You should spend about 20 minutes on this task.

> *Your neighbours have recently written to you to complain about the noise from your house/flat.*
>
> *Write a letter to your neighbours. In your letter*
> * *explain the reasons for the noise*
> * *apologise*
> * *describe what action you will take*

Write at least 150 words.

You do **NOT** need to write any addresses.

Begin your letter as follows:

Dear .... ,

WRITING TASK 2

You should spend about 40 minutes on this task.

Write about the following topic:

> *Some people believe that children are given too much free time. They feel that this time should be used to do more school work.*
>
> *How do you think children should spend their free time?*

Give reasons for your answer and include any relevant examples from your own knowledge or experience.

Write at least 250 words.

General Training: Reading and Writing Test B

SECTION 1　　*Questions 1–14*

Read the information below and answer Questions 1–7.

WALK FOR CHARITY

Dear Friend,

Please join us for our annual Walk for Charity. Starting in Weldown, you and your friends can choose a delightful 10, 20 or 30 kilometre route.

The money raised will provide support to help people all over the world. Start collecting your sponsors now and then simply come along on the day. Please read the instructions below carefully, especially if you require transport to and from Weldown.

See you on Sunday 14 May,

V Jessop

Walk Co-ordinator

P.S. Well done to last year's walkers for helping to raise a grand total of £21,000. The money has already been used to build a children's playground.

START TIMES:
30 km: 8 – 10 am
20 km: 8 – 10.30 am
10 km: 8 – 11.30 am

The organisers reserve the right to refuse late-comers.

CLOTHING should be suitable for the weather. If rain is forecast, bring some protection and be prepared for all eventualities. It is better to wear shoes that have been worn in, rather than ones that are new.

ROUTE MAPS will be available from the registration point. The route will be sign-posted and marshalled. Where the route runs along the road, walkers should keep to one side in single file, facing oncoming traffic at all times. If you need help along the route, please inform one of the marshals.

Free car parking available in car parks and on streets in Weldown.

BUSES

For the 10 and 20 km routes, a bus will be waiting at Fenton to take walkers back to Weldown. The bus will leave every half-hour starting at midday. The service is free and there is no need to book.

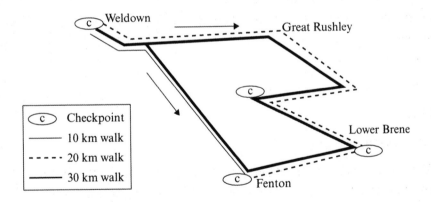

Questions 1–7

Look at the information on the previous page about a walk for charity.

*Answer the questions below using **NO MORE THAN THREE WORDS AND/OR A NUMBER** from the text for each answer.*

Write your answers in boxes 1–7 on your answer sheet.

1   What is the starting point for the 30 km walk?

2   What is the latest start time for the 20 km walk?

3   Regarding footwear, what are you warned against wearing?

4   What are the officials who help participants on the route called?

5   Where does the 20 km walk finish?

6   What is the frequency of the Fenton to Weldown bus?

7   Which walk does not pass through Lower Brene?

Questions 8–14

Read the information below and answer Questions 8–14.

The Week's Best

A
Wild Rose
(Tuesday 19.00)
This TV drama is about a young private detective employed by a team of New York businessmen who send her to Brazil to look into a series of hotel robberies. When she gets there, she discovers that the hotels, which are owned by the businessmen, have been empty for the last two years and the local authorities have no record of any robberies.

B
Animal Planet
(Wednesday 23.00)
This is a classic black-and-white film from the forties in which astronaut Charlie Huston crash-lands on a planet ruled entirely by animals. It is a first-class suspense adventure which also looks at the human condition, although this is not always a successful part of the film.

C
Strange Encounter
(Saturday 21.00)
Suspense is skilfully built up in this clever, small-scale supernatural story. A young couple view a deserted old house that they are interested in buying. They meet a strange old lady who tells them of the mystical powers of the house and how previous owners have been able to travel back through the centuries to meet their ancestors.

D
The Longest Walk
(Tuesday 21.30)
Ffyona Campbell is nearly there. All she has to do now is walk the length of France and Britain and she has succeeded in walking around the world. Tonight she drinks coffee in a tent and tells her story to Janet Street-Porter before she sets off for the Pyrenees mountains.

E
Rubicon 5
(Thursday 20.30)
This is a TV film being used to launch a new science fiction series. It has impressive special effects and a strong, believable cast of characters who travel to the twenty-third century. The action takes place in underground cities where the environment is controlled by computers.

F
New Science
(Friday 19.30)
This popular half-hour science magazine continues into its twenty-ninth year, proving itself to be a hardy survivor in the television world. Tonight it is presented by Carol Vorderman who introduces five reports, which include computer-driven cars and in-flight ten-pin bowling.

G
There and Back Again
(Sunday 22.00)
Paul Theroux's account of his recent journey from London to Japan and back makes ideal material for this evening's travel slot. Based on his own novel, the progress of his journey on the railways of Europe and Asia (Victoria station, Paris, Istanbul. . .) acts as a fascinating travelogue as the inhabitants gradually shift from the West to the East.

Questions 8–14

*Look at the seven television programmes **A–G** on the previous page and answer Questions 8–14.*

For which programme are the following statements true?

*Write the correct letter **A–G** in boxes 8–14 on your answer sheet.*

NB *You may use any letter more than once.*

  8   This programme is in the form of a personal interview.

  9   This programme is a documentary about technological developments.

10   These **TWO** programmes are about time travel.

11   This programme is taken from a book.

12   This film is the introduction to a set of programmes.

13   These **TWO** programmes are about present-day travellers.

14   This programme is about investigating a possible crime.

SECTION 2   *Questions 15–27*

Read the information below and answer Questions 15–20.

BINGHAM REGIONAL COLLEGE
International Students' Orientation Programme

What is it?

It is a course which will introduce you to the College and to Bingham. It takes place in the week before term starts, from 24th – 28th September inclusive, but you should plan to arrive in Bingham on the 22nd or 23rd September.

Why do we think it is important?

We want you to have the best possible start to your studies and you need to find out about all the opportunities that college life offers. This programme aims to help you do just that. It will enable you to get to know the College, its facilities and services. You will also have the chance to meet staff and students.

How much will it cost?

International students (non-European Union students)

For those students who do not come from European Union (EU) countries, and who are not used to European culture and customs, the programme is very important and you are strongly advised to attend. Because of this, the cost of the programme, exclusive of accommodation, is built into your tuition fees.

EU students

EU students are welcome to take part in this programme for a fee of £195, exclusive of accommodation. *Fees are not refundable.*

Accommodation costs (international and EU students)

If you have booked accommodation for the year ahead (41 weeks) through the College in one of the College residences (Cambourne House, Hanley House, the Student Village or a College shared house), you do not have to pay extra for accommodation during the Orientation programme.

If you have not booked accommodation in the College residences, you can ask us to pre-book accommodation for you for one week only (Orientation Programme week) in a hotel with other international students. The cost of accommodation for one week is approximately £165.

Alternatively, you can arrange your own accommodation for that week in a flat, with friends or a local family.

What is included during the programme?

Meals: lunch and an evening meal are provided as part of the programme, beginning with supper on Sunday 23rd September and finishing with lunch at midday on Friday 28th September. Please note that breakfast is not available.

Information sessions: including such topics as accommodation, health, religious matters, welfare, immigration, study skills, careers and other 'essential information'.

Social activities: including a welcome buffet and a half-day excursion round Bingham.

Transport: between your accommodation and the main College campus, where activities will take place.

Questions 15–20

Do the following statements agree with the information given in the text on the previous page?

In boxes 15–20 on your answer sheet, write

TRUE	*if the statement agrees with the information*
FALSE	*if the statement contradicts the information*
NOT GIVEN	*if there is no information on this*

15   Participants are advised to arrive one or two days early.

16   The cost of the programme for European Union students, excluding accommodation, is £195.

17   The number of places available is strictly limited.

18   Some students are not charged extra for accommodation during the programme.

19   The College will arrange accommodation with local families.

20   You can obtain breakfast at the College for an extra charge.

Read the information below and answer Questions 21–27.

Student Accommodation

The College offers five basic accommodation options. Here is some information to help you make your choice

A **CAMBOURNE HOUSE** – self-catering, student residence, located in the town centre about 2 miles from the main College campus. Up to 499 students live in 6, 7 and 8 bedroom flats, all with en-suite shower rooms. Rent is £64 per week, including bills (not telephone). Broadband Internet connections and telephones, with communal kitchen/dining and lounge areas. Parking space is available, with permits costing £60 per term.

B **STUDENT VILLAGE** – features 3, 4, 5 and 7 bedroom, self-catering shared houses for 250 students close to the main College campus. Rent is £60 per week inclusive of bills (except telephone). Parking is available with permits costing £90 for the academic year.

C **HANLEY HOUSE** – a second, modern, self-catering residence in the town centre for 152 students. Eighteen rooms per floor with communal kitchens, lounges, bathrooms and toilets. Rent is £53 per week including bills (not telephone). There is no space for parking nearby.

D **GLENCARRICK HOUSE** – a privately-owned and managed student residence in the town centre above a multi-storey car park, close to a major nightclub and housing 120 students. Rooms are allocated by the College Accommodation Service. Rents range from £58.50 to £68.50 for a single en-suite room or larger en-suite room respectively. A small extra charge is made for electricity.

E **HOUSE SHARES** – this recent initiative is a range of shared houses for 140 students, conforming to standards set by us to meet all legal safety requirements. A room in a shared house costs between £45 and £55 per week, exclusive of bills, and will be within a 4-mile radius of both campuses. As with halls of residence, the rent is payable termly.

Questions 21–27

Look at the accommodation options A–E on the previous page.

For which options are the following statements true?

Write the correct letter A–E in boxes 21–27 on your answer sheet.

NB *You may use any letter more than once.*

21 This is possibly inconvenient for car owners.

22 This is best if you like surfing the Web.

23 Of the College residences, this has the fewest students.

24 This is a new option offered by the College.

25 You have to organise parking a year at a time.

26 This accommodation does not belong to the College.

27 Here you definitely do not have your own bathroom.

SECTION 3   *Questions 28–40*

Read the passage below and answer Questions 28–40.

GLOW-WORMS

A

The glow-worm belongs to a family of beetles known as the Lampyridae or fireflies. The fireflies are a huge group containing over 2000 species, with new ones being discovered all the time. The feature which makes fireflies and glow-worms so appealing is their ability to produce an often dazzling display of light. The light is used by the adult fireflies as a signal to attract a mate, and each species must develop its own 'call-sign' to avoid being confused with other species glowing nearby. So within any one area each species will differ from its neighbours in some way, for example in the colour or pattern of its light, how long the pulses of light last, the interval between pulses and whether it displays in flight or from the ground.

B

The fireflies' almost magical light has attracted human attention for generations. It is described in an ancient Chinese encyclopaedia written over 2000 years ago by a pupil of Confucius. Fireflies often featured in Japanese and Arabian folk medicine. All over the world they have been the inspiration for countless poems, paintings and stories. In Britain, for example, there are plenty of anecdotes describing how glow-worms have been used to read by or used as emergency bicycle lamps when a cyclist's batteries have failed without warning. Early travellers in the New World came back with similar stories, of how the native people of Central America would collect a type of click beetle and release them indoors to light up their huts. Girls threaded them around their feet to illuminate the forest paths at night.

Fireflies very similar to those we see today have been found fossilised in rocks which were formed about 30 million years ago, and their ancestors were probably glowing long before then. It is impossible to be sure exactly when and where the first firefly appeared. The highest concentrations of firefly species today are to be found in the tropics of South America, which may mean either that this is where they first evolved, or simply that they prefer the conditions there.

Wherever they first arose, fireflies have since spread to almost every part of the globe. Today members of the firefly family can be found almost anywhere outside the Arctic and Antarctic circles.

C

As with many insects, the glow-worm's life is divided into four distinct stages: the egg, the larva (equivalent to the caterpillar of a butterfly), the pupa (or chrysalis) and the adult. The glow-worm begins its life in the autumn as a pale yellow egg. The freshly laid egg is extremely fragile but within a day its surface has hardened into a shell. The egg usually takes about 35 days to hatch, but the exact time varies according to the temperature, from about 27 days in hot weather to more than 45 days in cold weather. By the time it is due to hatch, the glow-worm's light organ is fully developed, and its glow signals that the egg will soon hatch.

After it has left the egg, the larva slowly grows from a few millimetres into the size and shape of a matchstick. The larval stage is the only time the insect can feed. The larva devotes much of its life to feeding and building up its food reserves so that as an adult it will be free to concentrate all its efforts on the task of finding a mate and reproducing. Throughout its time as a larva, approximately 15 months, the glow-worm emits a bright light. The larva's light is much fainter than the adult female's but it can still be seen more than five metres away.

In the final stage of a glow-worm's life, the larva encases itself in a pupal skin while it changes from the simple larva to the more complex adult fly. When the adult fly emerges from the pupa the male seeks a female with whom it can mate. After mating, the female lays about 120 eggs. The adult flies have no mouth parts, cannot eat and therefore only live a few days. When people talk of seeing a glow-worm they normally mean the brightly glowing adult female.

D

In some countries the numbers of glow-worms have been falling. Evidence suggests that there has been a steady decrease in the British glow-worm population since the 1950s and possibly before that. Possible causes for the decline include habitat destruction, pollution and changes in climate. Thousands of acres of grassland have been built upon and glow-worm sites have become increasingly isolated from each other. The widespread use of pesticides and fertilisers may also have endangered the glow-worm. Being at the top of a food chain it is likely to absorb any pollutants eaten by the snails on which it feeds. The effect of global warming on rainfall and other weather patterns may also be playing a part in the disappearance of glow-worms. A lot more research will be needed, however, before the causes of the glow-worm's gradual decline are clear.

E

Although glow-worms are found wherever conditions are damp, food is in good supply and there is an over-hanging wall, they are most spectacular in caves. For more than 100 years the glow-worm caves in New Zealand have attracted millions of people from all over the world. The caves were first explored in 1887 by a local Maori chief, Tane Tinorau, and an English surveyor, Fred Mace. They built a raft and, with candles as their only light, they floated into the cave where the stream goes underground. As their eyes adjusted to the darkness they saw myriad lights reflecting off the water. Looking up they discovered that the ceiling was dotted with the lights of thousands of glow-worms. They returned many times to explore further, and on an independent trip Tane discovered the upper level of the cave and an easier access. The authorities were advised and government surveyors mapped the caves. By 1888 Tane Tinorau had opened the cave to tourists.

Questions 28–33

The passage on the previous pages has five sections labelled **A–E**.

Which section mentions the following?

*Write the correct letter **A–E** in boxes 28–33 on your answer sheet.*

NB *You may use any letter more than once.*

28   threats to the glow-worm

29   ways in which glow-worms have been used

30   variations in type of glow-worm

31   glow-worm distribution

32   glow-worms becoming an attraction

33   the life-cycle of a glow-worm

Questions 34–40

Do the following statements agree with the information given in the passage?

In boxes 34–40 on your answer sheet, write

> **TRUE**   *if the statement agrees with the information*
> **FALSE**   *if the statement contradicts the information*
> **NOT GIVEN**   *if there is no information on this*

34   Scientists have only recently been able to list the exact number of glow-worm species.

35   The first fireflies appeared 30 million years ago.

36   Glow-worm populations are decreasing faster in some countries than in others.

37   Heat affects the production of glow-worm larvae.

38   Adulthood is the longest stage of a glow-worm's life.

39   The exact reason why glow-worm numbers are decreasing is unknown.

40   Glow-worms are usually found in wet areas.

WRITING

WRITING TASK 1

You should spend about 20 minutes on this task.

> *You have a full-time job and are also doing a part-time evening course. You now find that you cannot continue the course.*
>
> *Write a letter to the course tutor. In your letter*
>
> * *describe the situation*
> * *explain why you cannot continue at this time*
> * *say what action you would like to take*

Write at least 150 words.

You do **NOT** need to write any addresses.

Begin your letter as follows:

Dear .... ,

WRITING TASK 2

You should spend about 40 minutes on this task.

Write about the following topic:

> *Nowadays we are producing more and more rubbish.*
>
> *Why do you think this is happening?*
>
> *What can governments do to help reduce the amount of rubbish produced?*

Give reasons for your answer and include any relevant examples from your own knowledge or experience.

Write at least 250 words.

Tapescripts

SECTION 1

RECEPTIONIST:	Good afternoon, Dreamtime Travel. How can I help you?
CUSTOMER:	Oh hello. I'm interested in the holidays you offer along the coast near here.
RECEPTIONIST:	Yes. We operate several tours up the coast. Where in particular did you want to go?
CUSTOMER:	Well, I like the sound of the holiday that mentioned whales. Was it 'Whale Watching'?
RECEPTIONIST:	Oh, that's our <u>Whale Watch</u> Experience. It's very popular and it's based in a lovely little town with nice beaches.
CUSTOMER:	Oh right, and how long does it last?
RECEPTIONIST:	It's two days – that includes four hours' travel time each way from here.
CUSTOMER:	Good, I don't want to be away any longer than that. So is that by coach?
RECEPTIONIST:	Actually it's <u>by minibus</u>. We like to keep those tours small and personal so we don't take a whole coachload of people. In fact, we only take up to <u>fifteen people</u> on this tour, although we do run it with just twelve or thirteen.
CUSTOMER:	Oh, right. So do you run these tours often?
RECEPTIONIST:	Well it depends on the time of year. Of course in peak times like the summer holidays we do them every weekend, but at the moment it's usually once a month at most.
CUSTOMER:	And when is the next one going?
RECEPTIONIST:	Mmm, let me see. Um, there's one in three weeks' time which is <u>April the 18th</u>, and then we don't have another one until June the 2nd.
CUSTOMER:	All right, and is April a good time to go?
RECEPTIONIST:	Pretty good. Though the really good time is later in the year. I have to say though that the whale sighting is only one of the many things offered.
CUSTOMER:	Really?
RECEPTIONIST:	Yes. The hotel itself where you stay has great facilities. It's called The Pallisades.
CUSTOMER:	The Paris what?
RECEPTIONIST:	No, it's actually The Pallisades, <u>P-A-L-L-I-S-A-D-E-S</u>. It's right on the main beach there.
CUSTOMER:	Oh, I see.

The right-hand margin labels for the table above read, from top: *Example*, *Q1*, *Q2*, *Q3*, *Q4*.

RECEPTIONIST:	All of the rooms have nice views and the food is really good there too.
CUSTOMER:	Oh right.

CUSTOMER:	And what about the other things? You know, that are included in the price.	
RECEPTIONIST:	Oh, there are lots of things. If you don't want to do the whale watch cruise, your guide will take anyone who is interested either on <u>a bushwalk</u> through the national park near the hotel, and there's no extra charge for that, or on a fishing trip. That's an extra $12 I think. And there's also a reptile park in town – that costs more or less the same.	*Q5/Q6*
CUSTOMER:	No, I think I'd prefer whales to snakes.	
RECEPTIONIST:	Yeah. And if you just want to relax you are free to sit by the hotel pool or go down the beach. Oh, and they also have tennis courts at the hotel, but you have to pay for those by the hour. But there are <u>table tennis</u> tables downstairs and they're part of the accommodation package. Just speak to your guide.	*Q5/Q6*
CUSTOMER:	Well that sounds good. So how much is the basic tour price?	
RECEPTIONIST:	At this time of year it's usually around $300 but let me check. Er…oh, it's actually <u>$280</u>.	*Q7*
CUSTOMER:	And the next tour, are there any places on that one?	
RECEPTIONIST:	How many people is it for?	
CUSTOMER:	There are two of us.	
RECEPTIONIST:	Yes, that should be fine. Can I just mention that we require all bookings to be made at least <u>fourteen days</u> before you travel to avoid cancellations of tours. And if you cancel within seven days of departure you will have to pay 50% of your total booking.	*Q8*
CUSTOMER:	OK.	
RECEPTIONIST:	And you also need to pay a <u>20%</u> deposit at the time of booking.	*Q9*
CUSTOMER:	Can I pay that by credit card?	
RECEPTIONIST:	Yes, you can.	
CUSTOMER:	All right, what I'll do is I'll talk to my partner and get back to you.	
RECEPTIONIST:	Fine. So I'll make a provisional booking, shall I? – two for the Whale Watch Experience. Let me issue you with a customer reference number for when you call back. Do you have a pen?	
CUSTOMER:	Yes.	
RECEPTIONIST:	OK, it's <u>three nine seven, four five, T</u>. That's T for tango. When you call back, ask to speak to the Tour Manager, that's me, Tracy.	*Q10*
CUSTOMER:	Fine, I will.	

SECTION 2

Hello and welcome to today's 'Buyer Beware' programme, where we give you some tips on how to spend your money wisely. Now, in today's show we're looking at beds for children and babies. Let's start by looking at baby cots, that's for children of up to three years old. We tested three different cots all in the budget price range and, as usual, we will feature the good points, the problems and our verdict.

The first cot we looked at was by Baby Safe and it had several good points to recommend it. Our testers liked the fact that it had four wheels, so it was easy to <u>move around</u>. The only *Q11* slight problems with this cot were that it had no <u>brakes</u>, but they didn't think that mattered *Q12* too much. At first they were a bit concerned about the side bar, because they felt babies *Q13* could trap their <u>fingers</u> in it, but our testers felt that this was unlikely to happen so they have given this one a verdict of '<u>satisfactory</u>'. *Q14*

The next cot was by Choice Cots and this time our testers were pleased to find a cot which is simple to <u>put together</u> – unlike others we looked at. On the minus side, our testers did *Q15* not like the fact that the side of the cot did not drop down, making it difficult to pick up newborn babies. However, the real problem with this cot was the space between the bars; our testers found they were <u>too wide</u> and a baby could easily trap his head. We felt this *Q16* was a real safety hazard and so we have labelled this one <u>dangerous</u>, I'm afraid. *Q17*

And finally better news for the Mother's Choice cot. This cot was slightly different in that, although the side bar did not drop down, the base could be raised or lowered into two different positions making it safe as well as convenient. The negatives for this one were quite minor; the only niggle everyone had was the fact that it has no <u>wheels</u> and the only *Q18* other problem anyone could find, was that there were pictures which were simply stuck on and so could easily become detached. The makers have now promised to discontinue this practice. As this cot will then be safe in every way, we have made the Mother's Choice cot our <u>best buy</u>. Congratulations Mother's Choice! *Q19*

So, what features should you look for in a baby's cot? Well obviously safety is a very important factor as well as comfort and convenience. We recommend that, if you are buying a cot, do make sure that any metal present is not rusted or bent in any way. You should ensure your cot has only rounded or smooth edging without any <u>sharp</u> edges, *Q20* this is especially important for wooden cots.

And now on to beds for toddlers . . .

SECTION 3

ANDREW:	Excuse me, I was told to come here for advice about, erm, Management Diploma courses?
MONICA:	You've certainly come to the right place. Hi, my name is Monica.
ANDREW:	Nice to meet you. My name is Andrew, Andrew Harris.
MONICA:	So, Andrew, have you seen our diploma course prospectus yet?
ANDREW:	Yes, I've already looked at it. In fact, I thought the information on course content was really useful, but I'm afraid I'm a bit confused by all the different ways you can do the course: full-time intensive, part-time and so on.

MONICA:	Well, let's see if I can help. I think each course type has its advantages and disadvantages, so it really depends on you – your own study habits, and your financial circumstances, of course. Are you working at the moment?
ANDREW:	Yes. I've been working in the administration section of the local hospital for the last <u>three years</u>. And before that I worked in the office of a computer engineering company for two years. So, I've got about five years of relevant work experience. And what I'm hoping to focus on is Personnel Management.
MONICA:	I see. And are you planning to leave your current job to study, or are you thinking about just taking a year off?
ANDREW:	I want to know what my options are, really. I don't want to quit my job or anything and my employers are keen for me to get some more qualifications but obviously, it would be better if I could do a course without taking too much time away from work.
MONICA:	Right, so you don't really want to do the full-time course, then?
ANDREW:	No, not really. It's also a question of finances. You see, my office have agreed to pay <u>the cost of the course itself</u>, but I would have to take unpaid leave if I want to study full-time and, well, I don't think I could afford to support myself with no salary for a whole year.
MONICA:	OK. Well, you have two other possibilities: you could either do the part-time course – that would be over <u>two years</u> and you wouldn't have to take any time off work – or you could do what we call a 'modular' course. You could do that in eighteen months if you wanted – or longer, it's quite flexible and it would be up to you.
ANDREW:	Mmm. So what does the part-time course involve?
MONICA:	For that you would join an evening class and have a lecture twice a week. Then, you'd have to attend a seminar or discussion workshop one weekend a month.
ANDREW:	What kind of coursework would I have to do?
MONICA:	Well, it's a mixture. You'd be expected to write <u>an essay</u> each month, which counts towards your final assessment. You have a case study to do by the end of the course, which might involve doing a survey or something like that, and also you need to hand in <u>a short report</u> every four weeks.
ANDREW:	So, that's quite a lot of work, then, on top of working every day. It sounds like a lot of studying – and really tiring.
MONICA:	Yes, you certainly wouldn't have much free time!

Q21

Q22

Q23

Q24/Q25

Q24/Q25

ANDREW:	What about the 'modular' course? What would I have to do for that?
MONICA:	That's where you get the opportunity to study <u>full-time</u> for short periods. That way you can cover a lot of coursework and attend lectures and seminars during the day. And each module lasts for <u>one term</u>, say, about twelve weeks at a time. There are obvious advantages in this – the main one being that you can study in a much more <u>intensive</u> way, which suits some people much better.
ANDREW:	And how many of these 'modules' would I have to do to get the diploma?
MONICA:	The current programme is <u>two modules</u> – and then you have to choose <u>a topic</u> to work in more depth – but you can base that on your job, and so you don't need to be away from the office, and how long it takes is up to you.

Q26

Q27

Q28

Q29

Q30

The important thing is that you don't have to study and work. You can
focus on one thing at a time.

ANDREW: Yes, I can see that. It certainly sounds attractive! It would be more expensive,
though. I mean, I'd have to support myself without pay for each module.

MONICA: That's true, so that might be a problem for you. Look, why don't you talk this
over with your employers and . . .

SECTION 4

OK, so we've been looking at the attitudes of various social and cultural groups towards the
management of their personal finances – how important they feel it is to save money, and
what they save their money for. One aspect that we haven't yet considered is gender. So if we
consider gender issues we're basically asking whether men and women have different attitudes
towards saving money, and whether they save money for different things.

Back in 1928 the British writer George Bernard Shaw wrote in his *Intelligent Women's
Guide to Socialism and Capitalism* that 'A man is supposed to understand politics,   *Q31*
economics and finance and is therefore unwilling to accept essential instruction.' He also
said, 'A woman, having fewer pretensions, is far more willing to learn'. Now, though these   *Q32*
days people might question a lot of the assumptions contained in those statements, recent
research does suggest that there are some quite fundamental differences between men and
women in their attitudes to economic matters.

Let's look at what men and women actually save for. Research studies of women in
North America have found that women are far more likely to save for their children's   *Q33*
education and they are also more likely to save up in order to buy a house one day.
The same studies have found that men, on the other hand, tend to save for a car, which   *Q34*
by the way takes a surprisingly large amount of the household budget in North America.
But the other main priority for men when saving money is their retirement. When they're
earning, they're far more likely to put money aside for their old age than women are.

Now this is rather disturbing, because in fact the need for women to save for their old age
is far greater than for men. Let's consider this for a moment. To start with, it is a fact that
throughout the world, women are likely to live many years longer than men, so they need
money to support them during this time. Since women are likely to be the ones left
without a partner in old age, they may therefore have to pay for nursing care, because   *Q35*
they don't have a spouse to look after them. Furthermore the high divorce rates in
North America are creating a poverty cycle for women. It is the divorced women who
will most often have to look after the children and thus they need more money to look
after not just themselves but others.

So what can be done about this situation? The population in North America is likely to
contain an increasing number of elderly women. The research indicates that at present
for women it takes a crisis to make them think about their future financial situation.   *Q36*

But of course this is the very worst time for anyone to make important decisions. Women today need to look ahead, think ahead – not wait until they're under pressure. Even women in their <u>early twenties</u> need to think about pensions, for example, and with *Q37* increasing numbers of women in professional positions there are signs that this is beginning to happen. Then research also suggests that women avoid dealing effectively with their economic situation because of a lack of <u>confidence</u>. The best way for them to *Q38* overcome this is by getting themselves properly informed so they are less dependent on other people's advice. A number of initiatives have been set up to help them do this. This College, for example, is one of the educational institutions which offers night classes in <u>Money Management</u>, and increasing numbers of women are enrolling on such courses. *Q39* Here, they can be given advice on different ways of saving. Many women are unwilling to invest in stocks and shares, for instance, but these can be extremely profitable. It is usually advised that at least 70% of a person's savings should be in <u>low-risk investments</u> but for *Q40* the rest, financial advisors often advise taking some well-informed risks. Initiatives such as this can give women the economic skills and knowledge they need for a comfortable, independent retirement.

The increasing proportion of elderly women in the population is likely to have other economic consequences . . .

TEST 2

SECTION 1

LIBRARIAN:	Good morning, North College Library. How can I help you?
MAN:	I was wondering if it was possible to join the library.
LIBRARIAN:	Are you a student at North College?
MAN:	No, I'm not, but someone told me it was possible to join, even if I wasn't.
LIBRARIAN:	That's right, it is. Are you over <u>18</u>? That's our minimum joining age.
MAN:	Yes, I am.
LIBRARIAN:	That's no problem then.
MAN:	Could you tell me what I have to do to join?
LIBRARIAN:	Well, you'll need to come in to the library and fill out some forms. You'll also need to bring two <u>passport photos</u> with you. We also need two documents for ID, so a driving licence would be fine.
MAN:	I've got that and what else? A credit card?
LIBRARIAN:	No, it needs to have your address on it.
MAN:	Shall I bring <u>a bank statement</u>, would that do?
LIBRARIAN:	That'll be fine.
MAN:	Good. Does it cost anything to join?
LIBRARIAN:	Well, it's free for students here but otherwise it's <u>£125</u> per year or £25 if you've got a current student card from another college.
MAN:	I was at Westerley College until last year but now I've got a job at Jefferson's steel factory. Er, it's more expensive than I thought. My local library is free.

Example

Q1

Q2

Q3

133

LIBRARIAN:	But you'll find they don't have the range of reference books or facilities which we buy for our students. That's why you have to pay to be an external member.
MAN:	I see. How many books can I borrow?
LIBRARIAN:	We allow twelve items borrowed at any one time if you're a student, and that includes CDs, DVDs and videos. However, it's only <u>eight</u> items for members of the public.
MAN:	Fine. And how long can I have them for?
LIBRARIAN:	Well, you can have both fiction and reference books for four weeks which isn't bad really.
MAN:	And what happens if I return them late?
LIBRARIAN:	Like all libraries there's a fine system in place. The minimum fine is <u>£1.50</u> but it can be much higher for some items – up to £5 per week. We'll give you a booklet with all the details when you join. You can always renew items if they're not required by anyone else by telephoning or logging on to our website.

Q4

Q5

MAN:	What about the computers? Can I use them free of charge?
LIBRARIAN:	For college students it's free, but for external members like yourself, the first hour is free and then we make a nominal charge of £1 per hour thereafter.
MAN:	Do I have to book in advance for them?
LIBRARIAN:	Oh, yes, it's advisable. Most people tend to book twenty-four hours in advance although sometimes you can get one with only six hours' notice. However, the earliest you can book a computer is <u>forty-eight</u> hours before you need it, and you can only book one hour at a time. If no-one else has booked the computer out, then you may be able to have another hour if you want. We have a wide range of databases, so the computers are in great demand.
MAN:	I'm thinking of doing some writing and I might need to access national newspapers. Do you have them on these databases?
LIBRARIAN:	We do indeed. We've got all the big nationals, The Guardian and The Observer, The Independent and The Times and Sunday Times. We've also got all the <u>local papers</u> and a wide selection of magazines.
MAN:	Excellent. I assume you have photocopying facilities?
LIBRARIAN:	Of course. 5p a sheet for both A4 and A3 black-and-white copies and 40p a sheet for colour. You can get <u>a card</u> from the counter here – it doesn't take coins.
MAN:	OK. Oh by the way, another thing I was wondering about was if you ran any writing classes through the library?
LIBRARIAN:	We do, but you'll have to speak to John Grantingham about that. He's our resident author. He runs the creative writing classes.
MAN:	John . . . Grant . . . . Could you spell that for me please?
LIBRARIAN:	Certainly. <u>G - R - A - N - T - I - N - G - H - A - M</u>.
MAN:	Are the classes here at the library?
LIBRARIAN:	Yes – he's here on Thursday evenings, oh no sorry, <u>Friday</u> – he's just changed it. You can contact him by emailing the library.
MAN:	Okay. Right, well that's about all I need to know. Thank you. I'll be along later this week to join. Thanks. Bye.

Q6

Q7

Q8

Q9

Q10

SECTION 2

My name's Dan Pearman and I'd like to talk about the work of Pedal Power, a small charity based mainly in the UK. I'll be giving our contact details at the end, if anyone would like to find out more about how to support us.

But first, how the charity began. I got the idea of exporting bicycles to developing countries while I was in Ecuador. I went there in 1993 just after graduating from university. After three years of studying, I wanted adventure. I loved travelling, so <u>I decided to join a voluntary organisation</u> and was sent to Ecuador to carry out land surveys. The project came to an end after five years and when I returned to the UK in 1998, I started planning Pedal Power.   *Q11*

Where I lived in Ecuador was a very rural area. My neighbour had the only bicycle in the village, whereas everyone else walked everywhere. My neighbour's business was unusually successful, and for years I couldn't understand why. Then I realised <u>having a bike meant he could get where he wanted to go without much trouble</u>. Other local carpenters could only accept jobs in a three-kilometre radius, so no matter how skilled they were, they could never do as many jobs as my neighbour.   *Q12*

At Pedal Power, we collect second-hand bikes in the UK and send them to some of the poorest regions in the world. When we distribute bikes overseas we don't give them away for free. We'd like to, but long term that doesn't really help the local economy. The demand for bikes is enormous, which makes them very expensive locally. So we sell them for 5% of the normal price. <u>But in order to continue operating we need to have a constant supply of bikes which we send out every six months</u>.   *Q13*

One example of a town that's received bicycles from Pedal Power is Rivas. It was the first place I sent a full container of bicycles to. Most people there now own a bicycle. <u>The local economy has developed so much, you wouldn't recognise it as the same place</u>. In fact, there are more bikes than on the streets of Amsterdam, if you've ever been there.   *Q14*

But Pedal Power still needs your help. You may have read about some of our recent problems in the British media. In August 2000, we simply ran out of money. We had containers of bikes ready to send, but <u>no money to pay the bills</u>. It was a terrible situation. We managed to ensure the bikes went out on time, but the other problems carried on for several months.   *Q15*

Fortunately in October 2001 we won an Enterprise Award which helped us enormously. We invested fifteen of the <u>seventy-five-thousand-pound</u> prize money to help secure our future. Winning the award helped raise our profile, and the money enabled us to pay all our shipping costs, which represent our greatest expense. Pedal Power changes lives – when someone gets a bicycle from us, they see a 14% increase in their income. We're currently looking to invest in <u>computers</u> so that our office staff can do an even better job. Because of our work, people in a number of countries now have a better standard of living – so far   *Q16*

Q17

we've provided 46,000 people with bikes. But we'd like to send more, at least 50,000 by the end of the year.

Now there are many ways in which you can support the work of Pedal Power, not just by taking a bike to a collection in your area. I should also like to say if you do have a bike to donate, it doesn't matter what condition it's in – if we can't repair it, we'll strip it down for spare parts. Of course, to do that <u>we always need tools</u>, which are expensive to buy, so we welcome any that you can give. Also, you could help by contacting the voluntary staff at our offices, they'll be able to suggest <u>activities you could organise to bring in funds for us</u>. People do all kinds of things – including, of course, sponsored bike rides. Also, <u>we're always interested to hear of other places that would benefit from receiving a consignment of bikes</u>, and welcome suggestions from people who've been to developing regions on their travels. We hope that by talking on radio programmes like this, we will be able to raise public awareness, which will lead to government organisations also giving us regular financial support, something that we really need.

Q18/19/20

Q18/19/20

Q18/19/20

If you'd like some more information about where to donate an old bicycle or offer help in other ways please contact us on . . .

SECTION 3

TUTOR:	First of all I'd just like to say, Cristina and Ibrahim, that I really enjoyed watching your video about student life last week, and I could see that the rest of the group did too. You did really well, and I hope that you got a lot out of it. I'd like to use this tutorial as a feedback session, where you reflect on the experience of doing the project. So Cristina, I was wondering, what did you enjoy most about making the video?
CRISTINA:	I liked using the camera.
TUTOR:	Is it the first time you've operated one like that?
CRISTINA:	Yes, it is.
TUTOR:	Well the results were very good! Anything else?
CRISTINA:	I also enjoyed visiting one of the British students we filmed. I'd never been inside a British <u>home</u> before.
TUTOR:	OK Cristina, thanks. What about you, Ibrahim? What did you enjoy?
IBRAHIM:	Well for me it was a very good chance to get to know students who are on other courses, because everyone in our group is studying English, and we don't usually have much to do with the rest of the college.
TUTOR:	Yes, good. Do you think you'll maintain the contact now?
IBRAHIM:	I hope so. I've invited three of them to <u>have dinner</u> with me next week.
TUTOR:	Great! If you haven't decided what to make yet I can tell you they'll love trying Arab dishes. And of course, it's good for your English too. Cristina, what did you find? What was the most useful aspect of the project from the point of view of the English practice?

Q21

Q22

CRISTINA:	I think, when we were being shown how to edit the film, we had to follow the instructions. And that was very good practice for me. And I also learned some <u>technical</u> words that I hadn't heard before.
TUTOR:	What about you Ibrahim? What was the most useful for your English?
IBRAHIM:	It was listening to the British students, because they don't speak as slowly as most of the tutors on our course. I think they speak at natural speed, so it forces me to get used to it. And they use a lot of <u>slang</u>.
TUTOR:	So you learned some new words which will be useful?
IBRAHIM:	Yes.
TUTOR:	Good. I'm glad it helped. Well, we've talked a little bit about enjoyment, and about language practice. Were there any other benefits? What else did you feel you'd learnt from the project? Was it useful in other ways?
CRISTINA:	Yes, well firstly, I learned how to use a video camera. And also, I think I really learned a lot about working together with other people. I've never done anything with a group before, and we had to find ways of <u>cooperating</u>, erm, and compromising, and sometimes <u>persuading</u> people, when they don't agree with you.
TUTOR:	Yes, that is a very useful experience, I know.

Q23

Q24

Q25
Q26

TUTOR:	What about you, Ibrahim?
IBRAHIM:	Well, I think I learnt a lot about how important <u>editing</u> is. When you're filming you think that everything's going to be interesting, but in fact we cut around half of it in the end, and then it was much better.
TUTOR:	Good. Well, one last thing I'd like to ask. What mistakes do you think you, as a group that is, made? I mean, to put it another way, if you had to do it all over again, is there anything you'd do differently?
CRISTINA:	We didn't plan very well. For example, we didn't decide on dates when we'd <u>complete</u> each separate step of the project, and we should have agreed about that in the beginning, because we were always late with everything!
TUTOR:	Right. Anything else?
CRISTINA:	I think we should have tried to <u>experiment</u> more with the camera. I mean with angles, and the focus and that kind of thing.
TUTOR:	So you should have been more ambitious? Do you agree, Ibrahim?
IBRAHIM:	Not really. In fact, I think we were too ambitious. We were inexperienced, and we didn't have a lot of time, and we tried to do too much, to make a <u>long</u> film. Next time I would make a shorter one and try to get the quality better.
TUTOR:	Well, that's very interesting. Next semester we will be doing another video project – with a different content, of course – but you'll have an opportunity to put into practice what you've learnt this time. Do you have any ideas about . . .

Q27

Q28

Q29

Q30

SECTION 4

Tonight I'm going to talk to you about that remarkable continent Antarctica – remote, hostile and at present uninhabited on a permanent basis. For early explorers, it was the ultimate survival contest; for researchers like me, it remains a place of great intellectual challenge; while for the modern tourist, it's simply a wilderness of great beauty.

First, some facts and figures. Antarctica is a place of extremes – the highest, coldest and windiest continent and over <u>fifty-eight</u> times the size of the UK. The ice-cap contains almost 70% of the world's fresh water and 90% of its ice, but with very low snowfall, most of the continent technically falls unbelievably into the category of '<u>desert</u>'! Huge icebergs break off the continent each year, while in winter half the surrounding ocean freezes over, which means its size almost doubles.

Q31

Q32

Research and exploration has been going on in Antarctica for more than two hundred years, and has involved scientists from many different countries, who work together on research stations. Here <u>science</u> and technical support have been integrated in a very cost-effective way – our Antarctic research programme has several summers-only stations and two all-year-round ones; I was based on one of the all-year-round ones.

Q33

The research stations are really self-contained communities of about twenty people. There's living and working space, a kitchen with a huge food store, a <u>small hospital</u> and a well-equipped gym to ensure everyone keeps fit in their spare time. The station generates its own electricity and communicates with the outside world using a satellite link.

Q34

Our station – Zero One – had some special features. It wasn't built on land but on an ice-shelf, hundreds of metres thick. Supplies were brought to us on large sledges from a <u>ship</u> fifteen kilometres away at the ice edge.

Q35

Living in the Antarctic hasn't always been so comfortable. Snow build-ups caused enormous problems for four previous stations on the same site, which were buried and finally crushed by the weight. Fortunately no-one was hurt, but these buildings became a huge challenge to architects who finally came up with a remarkable solution – the buildings are placed on <u>platforms</u> which can be raised above the changing snow level on legs which are extendable.

Q36

Food is one of the most important aspects of survival in a polar climate. People living there need to obtain a lot more energy from their food, both to keep warm and to undertake heavy physical work. Maybe you know that an adult in the UK will probably need about 1,700 kilocalories a day on average; someone in Antarctica will need about <u>3,500</u> – just over double! This energy is provided by foods which are high in carbohydrate and fat.

Q37

Rations for fieldwork present an additional problem. They need to provide maximum energy, but they must also be compact and light for easy transport. Special boxes are prepared, each containing enough food for one person for twenty days. You may be familiar with coffee processed by freeze-drying, which preserves the quality of the food product while making a large saving in weight – well, this type of presentation is ideal in our situation. It wasn't available to earlier polar explorers, whose diet was commonly insufficient for their health.

I think that being at the cutting edge of science has a special appeal for everyone working in Antarctica, in whatever capacity. As a marine biologist, my own research was fascinating; but it's perhaps climate change research that is the most crucial field of study.

Within this general field, surveying changes in the volume and stability of the ice-cap is vital, since these may have profound effects on world sea levels and on <u>ocean currents</u>. *Q38* A second important area is monitoring the size of the hole in the ozone layer above Antarctica, since this is an indicator of global ultra-violet radiation levels. Thirdly, bubbles in the ice-sheet itself provide an index of <u>pollution</u> because frozen inside them are samples *Q39* of previous atmospheres over the past 500,000 years, and these provide us with evidence for the effects of such human activities as agriculture and industry.

There are an increasing number of opportunities for <u>young</u> people to work for a period in *Q40* Antarctica – not only as research assistants in projects like mine, but also in a wide range of junior administrative and technical positions including vacancies for map-makers. I hope that the insights I've provided will encourage you to take up these opportunities in this fascinating continent.

TEST 3

SECTION 1

MAN:	Good morning, please take a seat. How can I help you?
WOMAN:	Well, I'm thinking of buying a new car and I'd like some advice.
MAN:	Sure, yes. Had you got any particular make in mind?
WOMAN:	I'm interested in a <u>Lida</u> – I've had one before and liked it. But I haven't really made up my mind.

Example

MAN:	Sure. We've got various models. Umm, right. What about the engine size? Any ideas?
WOMAN:	The one I've got at the moment's a 1.2 litre engine but I find it a bit slow on long journeys. I'd like a bit more power this time . . . a <u>1.4</u> should do, I don't think I need a 1.6 or anything.

Q1

MAN:	Right. Well I think the model you're looking at is the Max. Here's a picture.
WOMAN:	Oh, yes . . . have you got one in?
MAN:	Yes. I'll take you to have a look at it in a minute. I'll just get a few more details. Er . . . Is there anything else to do with the engine? What kind of gear change do you want? I presume you'd want a manual?
WOMAN:	I'd want <u>automatic</u> – I've never driven a car with manual gears.

Q2

MAN:	Right. Well now, here's the colour chart for the Max. Have you given that any thought? This blue's very popular at the moment.

WOMAN:	Yes, it is nice, I like blue. What's it called? 'Royal'?	
MAN:	Yes.	
WOMAN:	But actually, I think I prefer this lighter shade here – '<u>Sky</u>'.	*Q3*
MAN:	Yes, that's popular too.	
WOMAN:	I think I'll go for that.	
MAN:	You might have to wait a week or so for that colour, but I assume that'd be OK?	
WOMAN:	Oh yes, fine.	
MAN:	Well, we can go outside and you can have a good look at one, and perhaps take it out. But first, can I just ask you about finance? The cash price is going to be somewhere in the region of seven and a half thousand. How would you like to pay? Are you in a position to pay cash, or would you need credit?	
WOMAN:	I'd like <u>credit</u> provided the terms are reasonable.	*Q4*
MAN:	Well you can discuss that with my colleague in a moment; we have various arrangements. And would you be interested in us taking your present car as part exchange?	
WOMAN:	Yes.	
MAN:	OK, fine. So I'll just need some details from you and then we can do a valuation . . . Is that OK?	
WOMAN:	Fine, yes.	

MAN:	Could I have your full name?	
WOMAN:	Wendy Harries, that's <u>H-A-double R-I-E-S</u>.	*Q5*
MAN:	And is that Mrs . . . Miss . . . Ms . . . ?	
WOMAN:	It's <u>Doctor</u>, actually.	*Q6*
MAN:	Oh, right. And your address?	
WOMAN:	20 Green Banks.	
MAN:	Is that 'Green' spelled as in the colour?	
WOMAN:	Yes, that's right.	
MAN:	OK.	
WOMAN:	Alton.	
MAN:	Is that <u>O-L-T-O-N</u>?	
WOMAN:	Not quite, it begins with an <u>A</u>, not an O.	*Q7*
MAN:	Oh yes, that's in Hampshire isn't it?	
WOMAN:	That's right.	
MAN:	And do you know your postcode?	
WOMAN:	Yes. It's GU8 9EW.	
MAN:	Do you have a daytime phone number?	
WOMAN:	Well, I work at the hospital but it's a bit difficult to get hold of me. I can give you a number just for <u>messages</u>, and then I'll get back to you when I can. Is that OK?	*Q8*
MAN:	That's fine.	
WOMAN:	It's 0-7-9-8-2-5-7-6-4-3.	
MAN:	Fine. And about the car you have now, what make is it?	
WOMAN:	It's a Conti.	

MAN:	Do you know the year or the model name?	
WOMAN:	I think it's 1996, and it's called a <u>Lion</u> – like the animal.	*Q9*
MAN:	Then it must be 1994, because they brought out the Fox after that.	
WOMAN:	Oh right, yes.	
MAN:	Mileage? Roughly?	
WOMAN:	I'm not sure. I know it's less than seventy thousand.	
MAN:	OK. What colour is it?	
WOMAN:	It's grey, metallic grey.	
MAN:	Right, and one last thing – what sort of condition would you say it's in?	
WOMAN:	I'd probably describe it as <u>reasonable</u>. Do you need to see it? It's parked outside.	*Q10*
MAN:	Not at the moment, no. Perhaps you could call in one day next week . . .	

SECTION 2

MAN: As I said earlier, there is I think at Rexford an excellent combination of
physical and geographical advantages – as well as having a rural setting and
still being close to central London, something that will certainly be of interest
to you is that <u>Rexford is just 35 minutes from London Airport</u>. At Rexford we   *Q11/Q12*
have a strong research capability. We came 7th out of 101 universities in last
year's research assessment, carried out by a government body and did
particularly well in your particular subjects, engineering and science. Actually
we got a top research grade of five for engineering, geography and computer
sciences. One further point – and I know from talking to you individually that
a number of you may be looking for some experience in industry after the
course – is that all our science and engineering research departments have
unusually <u>close relationships with industry in the area</u>. Anyway that's enough   *Q11/Q12*
sales talk from me . . . I'll just take a sip of this coffee that's just arrived, thank
you, and then I'll say something about what actually happens when you apply.

Right . . . Now if you do decide to make an application, what you do is send
it directly to me in my department. I will then immediately send confirmation
and the application process begins. Er . . . I'd like to say at this point that you
shouldn't worry if this process doesn't work all that quickly – I mean
occasionally there are postal problems, but most often the hold-up is caused by
<u>references</u> – the people you give as referees, shall we say, take their time to   *Q13*
reply. Anyway, it's absolutely normal for this process to take three to four
months. What I do in this period is keep in touch with you and reassure you
that things are moving along.

One of the ways we've devised to help you decide about applying as well as
later when you've been accepted . . . hopefully . . . is to put you in contact
with, if possible, a student from your own <u>country</u> who is at present studying   *Q14*
with us. What you can do is phone them up – we will, of course, liaise between
you – and discuss your concerns with them. That way you can get an objective
opinion of what you can expect if you come to live and study at Rexford – not
only the academic atmosphere but important details like what the leisure

facilities are like and whether the English <u>weather</u> and food are really as awful   *Q15*
as everybody says!

   If you decide you can face it, the contact can also help you just before you
leave, with tips on what to pack and that sort of thing. At the moment I think
we've got two second-year students and one postgraduate from this country.

   Now to move on to the other concerns you expressed earlier. At a UK
university – as I'm sure you know – you will be in an environment where
<u>independent learning is the norm</u>, which takes most students a while to adjust   *Q16*
to, and at a time when you will be separated from your normal surroundings
and, in most cases, your family. This can be a difficult time. But remember that
something like 25% of our student body are international students like
yourselves, and that there are several organisations in the university and city
whose main purpose is to offer help and ensure that your time with us is
enjoyable and useful.

   One or two of you touched on the subject of accommodation earlier. So I'll
just add a few points: it is the University's policy to give priority in the
allocation of residence places to three categories, and those are: visiting
students, exchange students and <u>new postgraduate students</u>. However, demand   *Q17*
exceeds supply, so there is still a need to put your name down early for campus
accommodation, particularly if your family is accompanying you. This means
that the earlier you decide whether you want to study with us . . . and so get
the procedure moving, the better it will be for everybody. Yes?

WOMAN: What if you would prefer to live outside the university?

MAN: If you're planning to live off-campus, you've got to sort things out even earlier.
As with everything in short supply, the good accommodation gets snapped up
months before the beginning of term – in other words <u>if you're starting in</u>   *Q18*
<u>October you need to be thinking about it in June or at the very latest July</u>. So
you do need to think very carefully about what you need, how much you can
afford to pay, well in advance. What you can't do is leave it until a few days
before the start of term. The agencies in town are pretty good – it's just a
matter of contacting them in good time. Of course, we have a full-time
accommodation officer available to help all students. She'll get in touch with
you when you're accepted – she's got plenty of contacts in the town and <u>will</u>   *Q19*
<u>deal with the agencies on your behalf</u>.

   One or two of you asked me earlier about your level of spoken English.
Obviously most of you have already achieved a lot – I wish I could speak your
language half as well. Having said that though, I'm afraid the lecturers will
make little or no allowance for the presence of non-native speakers in the
audience. So anything you can do to improve your spoken English – even
beyond the pretty high levels most of you have already reached – will help
make your stay with us that bit more fun for you. Some <u>extra practice before</u>   *Q20*
<u>you arrive</u> is worth more than . . . for example private lessons afterwards, when
you won't really have time. Oh . . . and one last thing before I invite further
questions: it's very important that you . . .

SECTION 3

ANNIE: Oh Ben – I just remembered I never filled in that form for Nick – did you do it?

BEN: The course feedback form?

ANNIE: Yes. If you want, we can do it together, I've got mine here.

BEN: Is that OK?

ANNIE: Yeah.

BEN: OK, let's have a look then. What do we have to do?

ANNIE: Let's fill in the top first, let's see, Course, Course code . . .

BEN: Er, it's Communication in Business.

ANNIE: OK, Communication . . . in . . . Business, I do know that, but what's the code?

BEN: CB16 something, CB162, isn't it?

ANNIE: Mmm, that's it, OK and dates, when did we start? I remember, my birthday's on
May 4th and it was the day after, it must have been <u>May 5th</u>.   *Q21*

BEN: Gosh, doesn't seem that long ago, does it?

ANNIE: No, and we finish at the end of this week, on Friday, so that's <u>July</u> 15th?   *Q22*

BEN: Er <u>16</u>th, Monday was the 12th. Right, that was the easy bit, now let's have a
look – "Please give your comments on the following aspects of the course",
OK, what's the first one? Oh, course organisation. What do you think?

ANNIE: Er, clear? It was, wasn't it?

BEN: Yes, I think the organisation <u>was clear</u>. OK, anything else for course organisation?   *Q23*

ANNIE: It was a good thing he gave us <u>the course outline</u> at the beginning, in the first   *Q24*
session, that was useful, so I'll put that down, shall I? Now, going on to suggestions
for improvement, one thing that wasn't so good, I think we could have done a bit
more work at the beginning, I mean at the beginning it seemed dead easy.

BEN: Yeah.

ANNIE: I thought it was going to be really easy and then all of a sudden in the <u>second</u>   *Q25*
<u>half</u> of the course we got a whole load of work, reading to do and essays and
things.

BEN: Yes, it'd be better if it was more even. OK, now course delivery, does that mean
teaching?

ANNIE: Yeah, I suppose so. Well, what I thought was really good on this course was the
<u>standard of teaching</u>. Actually – I mean some of the teachers were better than   *Q26*
others – but the standard generally was fine. Much better than other courses I've
been on.

BEN: Yeah, I agree. Let's put that then. What about suggestions for improvement?

ANNIE: I . . . I didn't think it was all that wonderful when we had great long <u>group</u>   *Q27*
<u>discussion</u> sessions that went on for hours and hours. I don't mean we shouldn't
have group discussions, just that they shouldn't go on too long.

ANNIE: Now, on to materials and equipment.

BEN: Oh, now what was good about some sessions was the <u>handouts.</u>   *Q28*

ANNIE: Yes, I thought all the handouts were good actually, and some were great, with
website addresses and everything.

BEN: One problem though with materials was the key texts.

ANNIE: Yes! There just weren't enough copies on reserve in the library. And if you can't get the key texts before the session, how are you supposed to do the reading? And not enough computers. You have to wait ages to get one.

BEN: OK, testing and evaluation – well, I don't know, it's hard to say until we've got our written assignments back.

ANNIE: Don't talk about it, I only got mine in yesterday, it was a real struggle. I hate to think what mark I'll get.

BEN: Yes, but at least we've done the oral presentation – I thought that was good, the way I got my feedback really quickly.

ANNIE: Yes, it was. And I liked the way we knew what we'd be evaluated on, we knew the criteria, so we knew we had to think about clarity, organisation, and so on.

BEN: Yeah, but I'm not so sure about the <u>written work</u>. One thing I think is that there's just too much, it's really stressful.   *Q29*

ANNIE: Yes, I'd agree and I don't see why they can't let us know the criteria they use for marking.

BEN: The written assignments? But he told us.

ANNIE: No, for the final exams. What are they looking for – what are the criteria? What makes a pass or a fail?

BEN: Yeah, I never thought of that. It'd be really useful.

ANNIE: OK, any other comments?

BEN: I thought <u>student support</u> was excellent.   *Q30*

ANNIE: Yeah, me too. OK, excellent. Other comments?

BEN: No, I can't think of anything else.

ANNIE: Nor me. OK, so that's done. Thanks, Ben.

BEN: No, thank you.

SECTION 4

STUDENT: Well, my group has been doing a project on how household waste is recycled in Britain.

We were quite shocked to discover that only 9% of people here in the UK make an effort to recycle their household waste. This is a lower figure than in most other European countries, and needs to increase dramatically in the next few years if the government is going to meet its recycling targets.

The agreed targets for the UK mean that by 2008 we must reduce our carbon dioxide emissions by <u>12.5%</u>, compared with 1990. And recycling can   *Q31*
help to achieve that goal, in two main ways: the production of recycled glass and paper uses much less energy than producing them from virgin materials, and also recycling reduces greenhouse gas emissions from landfill sites and <u>incineration plants</u>.   *Q32*

As part of our project, we carried out a survey of people in the street, and the thing that came up over and over again is that people don't think it's easy enough to recycle their waste. One problem is that there aren't enough '<u>drop-off</u>' sites, that is, the places where the public are supposed to take their waste.   *Q33*

We also discovered that waste that's collected from householders is taken to places called 'bring banks', for sorting and baling into loads. One problem here is taking out everything that shouldn't have been placed in the recycling containers: people put all sorts of things into bottle banks, like plastic bags and even broken umbrellas. All this has to be removed by hand. Another difficulty is that toughened glass used for <u>cooking</u> doesn't fully melt at the temperature required for other glass, and so that also has to be picked out by hand.

Q34

Glass is easy to recycle because it can be reused over and over again without becoming weaker. Two million tons of glass is thrown away each year, that is, seven billion bottles and jars; but only <u>500,000</u> tons of that is collected and recycled.

Q35

Oddly enough, half the glass that's collected is green, and a lot of that is imported, so more green glass is recycled than the UK needs. As a result, new uses are being developed for recycled glass, particularly green glass, for example in fibreglass manufacture and water filtration. A company called CLF Aggregates makes a product for <u>roads</u>, and 30% of the material is crushed glass.

Q36

For recycling paper, Britain comes second in Europe with 40%, behind Germany's amazing 70%.

When recycling started, there were quality problems, so it was difficult to use recycled paper in office printers. But these problems have now been solved, and Martin's, based in South London, produces a range of office stationery which is 100% recycled, costs the same as normal paper and is of equally high quality.

But this high quality comes at a cost in terms of the waste produced during the process. Over a third of the waste paper that comes in can't be used in the recycled paper, leaving the question of what to do with it. One firm, Papersave, currently sells this to farmers as a <u>soil conditioner</u>, though this practice will soon be banned because of transport costs and the smell, and the company is looking into the possibility of alternative uses.

Q37

Plastic causes problems, because there are so many different types of plastic in use today, and each one has to be dealt with differently. Pacrite recycles all sorts of things, from bottles to car bumpers, and one of its most successful activities is recycling plastic bottles to make <u>containers</u> which are used all over the country to collect waste.

Q38

The Save-a-Cup scheme was set up by the vending and plastics industries to recycle as many as possible of the three-and-a-half billion polystyrene cups used each year. At the moment 500 million polycups are collected, processed and sold on to other businesses, such as Waterford, which turns the cups into <u>pencils</u>, and Johnson & Jones, a Welsh-based firm, which has developed a wide variety of items, including <u>business cards</u>.

Q39
Q40

Well, to sum up, there seems to be plenty of research going on into how to re-use materials, but the biggest problem is getting people to think about recycling instead of throwing things away. At least doing the research made us much more careful.

TEST 4

SECTION 1

ADVISER: Good morning, how can I help you?

STUDENT: Good morning. Umm, I understand you help fix up students with host families.

ADVISER: That's right . . . are you interested in . . .?

STUDENT: Yes . . .

ADVISER: Well please sit down and I'll just take a few details.

STUDENT: Thank you.

ADVISER: Right now . . . what name is it?

STUDENT: Jenny Chan.

ADVISER: Can you spell that please?

STUDENT: Yes . . . <u>J-E-N-N-Y C-H-A-N</u>.   *Example*

ADVISER: Right . . . and what is your present address?

STUDENT: Sea View Guest House, <u>14 Hill Road</u>.   *Q1*

ADVISER: OK, and do you know the phone number there?

STUDENT: Yes . . . I have it here, ummm . . . 2237676, but I'm only there after about 7 pm.

ADVISER: So when would be the best time to catch you?

STUDENT: I suppose <u>between 9 and, let me see, half-past</u>, before I leave for the college.   *Q2*

ADVISER: Great . . . and can I ask you your age?

STUDENT: I've just had my nineteenth birthday.

ADVISER: And how long would you want to stay with the host family?

STUDENT: I'm planning on staying <u>a year</u> but at the moment I'm definitely here for   *Q3*
             four months only. I have to get an extension to my permit.

ADVISER: You're working on it? Fine . . . and what will be your occupation while
             you're in the UK?

STUDENT: Studying English?

ADVISER: And what would you say your level of English is?

STUDENT: Umm. Good, I think I'd like to say 'advanced' but my written work is
             below the level of my spoken, so I suppose it's <u>intermediate</u>.   *Q4*

ADVISER: Certainly your spoken English is advanced. Anyway, which area do you
             think you would prefer?

STUDENT: Ummm, well I'm studying right in the centre but I'd really like to live in
             the <u>north-west</u>.   *Q5*

ADVISER: That shouldn't be a great problem . . . we usually have lots of families up
             there.

- -

ADVISER: And do you have any particular requirements for diet?

STUDENT: Well, I'm nearly a <u>vegetarian</u> . . . not quite.   *Q6*

ADVISER: Shall I say you are? It's probably easier that way.

STUDENT: That would be best.

ADVISER:	Anything about your actual room?	
STUDENT:	I would prefer my own facilities – 'en suite', is that right? And also if it's possible a TV and I'd also like the house to have <u>a real garden</u> rather than just a yard, somewhere I could sit and be peaceful.	*Q7*
ADVISER:	Is that all?	
STUDENT:	Well . . . I'm really serious about improving my English so I'd prefer to be <u>the only guest</u> if that's possible?	*Q8*
ADVISER:	No other guests . . . Yes, you get more practice that way. Anyway, obviously all this is partly dependent on how much you're willing to pay. What did you have in mind?	
STUDENT:	I was thinking in terms of about £60–£80 a week, but I'd go up to <u>a hundred</u> if it was something special.	*Q9*
ADVISER:	Well I don't think we'd have any problems finding something for you.	
STUDENT:	Oh, good.	
ADVISER:	And when would you want it for?	
STUDENT:	I'd like to move in approximately two weeks.	
ADVISER:	Let me see, it's the 10th today . . . so if we go for the <u>Monday</u> it's the <u>23rd March</u>.	*Q10*
STUDENT:	Yes.	
ADVISER:	Right . . . good, and if I could ask one last question . . .	

SECTION 2

Good evening everyone and thank you for coming to the Soccer Club meeting. It's good to see so many parents and children here tonight, and I know you are looking forward to a great football season. Now I'd like to take a few minutes to tell you about some changes to the Soccer Club for the coming season.

Now, this season we'll be playing all our matches for both the junior and senior competitions at King's Park, instead of Royal Park, which was used last season.

Now for meetings, we're going to use the <u>clubhouse</u> in King's Park, and the next meeting   *Q11*
will be held in the clubhouse on the 2nd of July.

As usual, we hope to begin the season with a <u>picnic</u> next Saturday at the clubhouse. Please   *Q12*
try and come to the picnic as it's always good fun. The last week of the season we usually
have a dinner and presentation of <u>prizes</u> to the players, and more information about this   *Q13*
will be given to you later in the season.

This season we have more teams than ever. We hope to have <u>ten</u> teams, instead of five, in   *Q14*
the junior competition and they will play on Saturday mornings, beginning at 8.30 a.m.
Training sessions will be held in King's Park on <u>Wednesday afternoons</u> for the juniors   *Q15*
and they will be wearing red shirts again this year.

In the senior competition, there'll be <u>four</u> teams, the same as last year, and their games will   *Q16*
be played on Saturday afternoons starting at 2.30, no sorry, it will be a 2 o'clock start, and
the training session for seniors is planned for <u>Sunday afternoons</u>.   *Q17*

Now I'd like to introduce you to the new committee for the Soccer Club for this season.
Firstly, let me welcome Robert Young, the new President, who will manage the meetings for
the next two years. Robert's son has been playing football with the club for over five years
now, and many thanks to Robert for taking on the job of President.

Next we have Gina Costello, she's the treasurer, and she will <u>collect the fees</u> from you for   *Q18*
the season. Please try and give Gina your fees as early as possible in the season, as the
club needs the money to buy some new equipment.

Then there's David West who has volunteered to be the club secretary, and one of the many
jobs he will have is to <u>send out newsletters</u> to you regularly. If you have any information   *Q19*
that may be useful, please let David know so that it can be included in these newsletters.

Also I'd like to introduce you to Jason Dokic who is the Head Coach. For all the new
members here tonight, this is the third year that Jason has been with us as Head Coach,
and we are very lucky to have such an experienced coach and former player at our club.
He will continue to <u>supervise the teams</u>, at training sessions and on match days.   *Q20*

Now before we finish and have some refreshments, does anyone have any questions
they'd like to ask the new committee?

SECTION 3

TUTOR: Right, Jason and Karin, now I asked you to look at the case study for Box
Telecom as part of your exam assessment. It's interesting because they are in the
middle of problems at the moment and I want you to track how they deal with
them. Let's start with you, Karin. Having read through the case study, can you
just summarise what the problems were that Box Telecom had to take on board?

KARIN: Um, yeah . . . Well of course what first came to their attention was that, despite
a new advertising campaign, they were suffering from falling <u>sales</u> – and this is   *Q21*
something that had many causes. On top of that immediate problem, what had
also happened over the last two years was that, although they had invested in an
expansion plan, they had to face up to increased <u>competition</u>. And, before they   *Q22*
had a chance to get to grips with the effects of that, they were stalled by a strike
and it was just when they were thinking about making a colossal investment in
new machinery for their plants. So they were really in trouble.

TUTOR: Yes, I think that's fair. And Jason, you contacted the company, didn't you?
What did the company define as the reasons for these problems?

JASON: Well, I think they've hit on the right things – it would be easy to say they had invested too heavily, or at the wrong time, but in fact the signs were good and what they were set back by was high <u>interest rates</u>. At the same time, their *Q23* longer-term problems, which were affecting their market share, were eventually credited to poor <u>training</u> – and having looked at the details in their last report *Q24* I think that's right.

TUTOR: So, onto the larger issues then. Karin, what do you think the company will do?

KARIN: Hmm . . . Well, obviously they have the choice of accepting the very favourable terms that another company – KMG Plc – have given them to buy them out. That would mean creating a new company with a new image. Or they could decide on a bolder move and offer some new shares if they wanted. But I think they're much more cautious than that and expect they will start <u>trying to find</u> *Q25* <u>individuals who'd be prepared to back them with some of the capital they need</u>.

TUTOR: Well, you mustn't always assume that dramatic problems require dramatic solutions. Sometimes there's a simple fix such as changing the guy at the top. If they truly are cautious, then I suspect they will seek to shut down some of their shops. But a more ambitious approach, and one which I think would have more chance of success, would be to <u>alter how they're running things</u> – the *Q26* management layers and the processes. So in your analysis try to think of all the options. Jason?

JASON: Yes, it's interesting because I've found it a really useful company to study. Its problems cross all types of industries and it's lucky it's so big – a smaller or even medium-sized company would have gone under by now.

TUTOR: Ah well in fact, what I want you two to do is to go away when we've finished our discussion today and write a report. We've looked in general at the telecommunications market in the UK over the last few sessions and I want you to take Box Telecom as an example and <u>suggest some ways in which</u> *Q27* <u>they might overcome their problems</u>. And outline the reasons why you think as you do – but try and keep it intrinsic to the company rather than dragging in other examples. Is that OK, Karin?

KARIN: Yes, I think I can do that. Personally I've got great hopes for it. <u>I think it</u> *Q28* <u>will recover</u>. That advertising campaign they did was very strong and they're very innovative with their products – they set new trends. The company's got to recover, don't you think, Jason?

JASON: Hmmm – I'm not sure. I think it can but it's not a foregone conclusion unless they manage <u>to attract the right level of investment. The company definitely</u> *Q29* <u>needs a boost</u> and to attract more highly skilled workers if their recovery is to be long-lasting. When I was talking to the marketing manager he said to me that he thinks the company had got a great management team – but he would say that, wouldn't he? – but they are suffering from having to work with outdated production machinery and that could cost a lot to put right.

TUTOR: Well, personally I think the stock market is to blame. I think they were expecting too much of the company and then inevitably it looked bad when it didn't perform. The market should have had more realistic expectations.

And I disagree with you about the advertising campaign Karin. That's   Q30
where they could do with some innovation – to get sales kick-started.
Anyway, let's see what you come up with . . . *[fade]*

SECTION 4

OK, are you all settled? Well, first of all, welcome to Cardiff University. I'm here to explain
what we can offer you.

Now, as a new student at the university, you will probably need some sort of guidance to
help you to use the library effectively to study and research. Some of you have asked
about a guided tour but we find this rather muddles people. So, in this first week, we run a   Q31
series of talks which focus on different aspects of the library and its resources. You'll also
find that to get the most out of the library you really do need to be computer literate and
so all this term we run small classes which will bring you up to speed on how to access the
computer-loaded information.

OK, now let me give you an outline of what's available to you. You'll find that the computers
are increasingly used as a research tool. Many students do most of their research on the
internet and the library computers are permanently online. Having found what you need,
you'll find you can readily save texts on your personal computer space to print off when
you need. You might think that it is the fastest way to get information but the links can
be slow. Clearly you can find lots on there but much of it is useless information as it is   Q32
from highly debatable sources – so be critical. You'll also find that the library has loaded
several CD-ROMS onto the computers from specialist reference sources such as the MLA.
It means we can expand what we offer you at very little extra cost and saves us having to   Q33
invest in more and more books. The CD-ROMS contain exactly the same information as
the reference books as the two are updated together.

Now most of you will need to refer to journal articles in your work and you'll find you can
also access these online and we encourage you to do so.

Clearly some of you will find the printed version more accessible as it sits on the shelves but   Q34
I'm afraid the intention is to phase these out eventually. However, you will still be able to
print off a version of the text rather than photocopying the journal pages. So you must get
used to working online. Naturally we do still have the full range of classic reference books,
additional to the CD-ROMS, for you to use and there are several copies of each one. This is
because some of you may prefer to borrow a book rather than sit in the library. There is a   Q35
restricted loan time on these so that they are not missing from the shelves for too long.
Although there is a Section Manager for each part of the library, they are very busy and so,
if you do get stuck looking for things, you should ask the relevant Cataloguing Assistant.
As your Training Supervisor, I just oversee your induction and will not be around after   Q36
this initial week.

Some of you may be interested to know that the library is offering specialised training sessions on writing a dissertation. Obviously this is not relevant to those of you who are undergraduates; it is just for postgraduates. Your department will discuss the planning stage of the dissertation – i.e. what you're going to do – with you and we will focus on the structure of it. However, the training will also include some time on the computers. *Q37*
I realise most of you know how to organise files but we can show you the different *Q37*
ways to run data programmes. Your tutors will tell you at the outset how to set out the chapters they require but you will need to ask them how they would like you to organise *Q38*
the bibliography because it varies depending on your subject area. When you've got *Q39*
something together the trainer here will look through the draft version for you to see if it's OK. And, one final point, for those of you who have registered from abroad, we can offer individual sessions on dissertations if you feel you need them. If you *Q40*
require language lessons then they are available from the International Centre next to the Law Department.

Answer key

TEST 1

LISTENING

Section 1, Questions 1–10

1   by minibus / a minibus
2   15 / 15 people
3   April (the) 18th
4   Pallisades
5–6   IN EITHER ORDER
    B
    D
7   280
8   14
9   20 %
10 39745T

Section 2, Questions 11–20

11 move around / move about
12 brakes
13 fingers
14 satisfactory
15 put (it) together
16 too wide
17 dangerous
18 wheels
19 (the) best / (the) best buy / safe
20 sharp

Section 3, Questions 21–30

21 B
22 A
23 C
24 & 25   IN EITHER ORDER
    B
    D
26 full-time
27 a term / one term
28 intensive
29 two modules / (for) two terms
30 a topic / one topic

Section 4, Questions 31–40

31 politics
32 learn
33 children's education / their children's education
34 a car
35 nursing care
36 crisis
37 early twenties
38 confidence
39 money management
40 low-risk investments

If you score . . .

0–13	14–28	29–40
you are highly unlikely to get an acceptable score under examination conditions and we recommend that you spend a lot of time improving your English before you take IELTS.	you may get an acceptable score under examination conditions but we recommend that you think about having more practice or lessons before you take IELTS.	you are likely to get an acceptable score under examination conditions but remember that different institutions will find different scores acceptable.

ACADEMIC READING

Reading Passage 1, Questions 1–13

1–3 *IN ANY ORDER*
 D
 E
 G
4 clerks / copying clerks
5 library ·
6 stability
7 pension
8 TRUE
9 FALSE
10 NOT GIVEN
11 FALSE
12 FALSE
13 TRUE

Reading Passage 2, Questions 14–26

14 F
15 A
16 B
17 D
18 I
19 C

20 B
21 D
22 C
23 NOT GIVEN
24 TRUE
25 FALSE
26 FALSE

Reading Passage 3, Questions 27–40

27 YES
28 NOT GIVEN
29 NO
30 NOT GIVEN
31 YES
32 NO
33 C
34 D
35 C
36 B
37 B
38 E
39 D
40 I

If you score . . .

0–11	12–29	30–40
you are highly unlikely to get an acceptable score under examination conditions and we recommend that you spend a lot of time improving your English before you take IELTS.	you may get an acceptable score under examination conditions but we recommend that you think about having more practice or lessons before you take IELTS.	you are likely to get an acceptable score under examination conditions but remember that different institutions will find different scores acceptable.

LISTENING

Section 1, Questions 1–10

1 (passport) photos / (passport) photographs
2 (a) bank statement
3 125 (per year)
4 8
5 1.50
6 48
7 local papers / local newspapers
8 (a) card / cards
9 Grantingham
10 Friday

Section 2, Questions 11–20

11 C
12 C
13 A
14 C
15 A
16 £75,000
17 computers
18–20 IN ANY ORDER
      C
      E
      F

Section 3, Questions 21–30

21 home / student's home
22 (have) dinner / come to dinner / go to dinner
23 technical
24 slang
25 cooperating / cooperation
26 persuading
27 editing
28 complete
29 experiment
30 long

Section 4, Questions 31–40

31 58
32 desert
33 science
34 hospital / small hospital
35 ship
36 platforms
37 3,500
38 currents / ocean currents
39 (the) pollution
40 young

If you score . . .

0–12	13–27	28–40
you are highly unlikely to get an acceptable score under examination conditions and we recommend that you spend a lot of time improving your English before you take IELTS.	you may get an acceptable score under examination conditions but we recommend that you think about having more practice or lessons before you take IELTS.	you are likely to get an acceptable score under examination conditions but remember that different institutions will find different scores acceptable.

ACADEMIC READING

Reading Passage 1, Questions 1–13

1 candlewax
2 synthetic
3 chemistry
4 Novalak
5 fillers
6 hexa
7 raw
8 pressure
9 B
10 C
11 TRUE
12 FALSE
13 FALSE

Reading Passage 2, Questions 14–27

14 FALSE
15 NOT GIVEN
16 TRUE
17 FALSE
18 TRUE
19 NOT GIVEN
20 TRUE
21 problem solving
22 temporal lobes
23 evaluating information
24 C
25 A
26 F
27 D

Reading Passage 3, Questions 28–40

28 Latin
29 doctors
30 & 31 *IN EITHER ORDER*
        technical vocabulary
        grammatical resources
32 Royal Society
33 German
34 industrial revolution
35 NOT GIVEN
36 FALSE
37 TRUE
38 popular
39 Principia / the Principia / Newton's Principia / mathematical treatise
40 local / more local / local audience

If you score . . .

0–12	13–29	30–40
you are highly unlikely to get an acceptable score under examination conditions and we recommend that you spend a lot of time improving your English before you take IELTS.	you may get an acceptable score under examination conditions but we recommend that you think about having more practice or lessons before you take IELTS.	you are likely to get an acceptable score under examination conditions but remember that different institutions will find different scores acceptable.

C 5 **TEST 3**

LISTENING

Section 1, Questions 1–10

1 1.4 litres / 1.4 liters
2 automatic
3 light / sky
4 credit
5 Harries
6 Dr / Doctor
7 Alton
8 messages
9 Lion
10 reasonable

Section 2, Questions 11–20

11 & 12 *IN EITHER ORDER*
     C
     E
13 references
14 country
15 weather
16 C
17 C
18 A
19 B
20 C

Section 3, Questions 21–30

21 5th May
22 16th July / Friday 16th July
23 clear / was clear
24 (an/the) outline / (a/the) course outline
25 (the) 2nd half
26 (standard of) teaching / (standard of) teachers
27 discussion / group discussion
28 handouts
29 written work
30 student support / support for students

Section 4, Questions 31–40

31 12.5 %
32 incineration plants
33 drop-off
34 cooking
35 500,000
36 roads
37 soil conditioner
38 containers
39 pencils
40 business cards

If you score . . .

0–13	14–28	29–40
you are highly unlikely to get an acceptable score under examination conditions and we recommend that you spend a lot of time improving your English before you take IELTS.	you may get an acceptable score under examination conditions but we recommend that you think about having more practice or lessons before you take IELTS.	you are likely to get an acceptable score under examination conditions but remember that different institutions will find different scores acceptable.

ACADEMIC READING

Reading Passage 1, Questions 1–13

1	D
2	B
3	C
4	E
5	B
6	D
7	A
8	B
9	D
10	C
11	TRUE
12	FALSE
13	NOT GIVEN

Reading Passage 2, Questions 14–26

14	iv
15	i
16	v
17	viii
18	YES
19	NOT GIVEN
20	NO
21	YES
22	NOT GIVEN
23	YES
24	F
25	A
26	B

Reading Passage 3, Questions 27–40

27	E
28	B
29	A
30	F
31	B
32	NOT GIVEN
33	FALSE
34	NOT GIVEN
35	TRUE
36	FALSE
37	TRUE
38	B
39	A
40	D

If you score . . .

0–11	12–28	29–40
you are highly unlikely to get an acceptable score under examination conditions and we recommend that you spend a lot of time improving your English before you take IELTS.	you may get an acceptable score under examination conditions but we recommend that you think about having more practice or lessons before you take IELTS.	you are likely to get an acceptable score under examination conditions but remember that different institutions will find different scores acceptable.

TEST 4

LISTENING

Section 1, Questions 1–10

1 14 Hill Road
2 between 9 and 9.30 / 9–9.30
3 1 year
4 intermediate
5 North-West
6 vegetarian
7 (a) (real) garden
8 (the) only guest
9 100
10 23rd March / Monday 23rd March

Section 2, Questions 11–20

11 clubhouse
12 picnic
13 prizes
14 10
15 Wednesday afternoon(s)
16 4
17 Sunday afternoon(s)
18 collect (the) fees / collect (the) money
19 send (out/the) newsletter(s)
20 supervise (the) teams

Section 3, Questions 21–30

21 sales
22 competition
23 interest rates / rates of interest
24 training
25 A
26 B
27 A
28 C
29 B
30 D

Section 4, Questions 31–40

31 B
32 A
33 A
34 C
35 A
36 B
37 B
38 A
39 B
40 C

If you score . . .

0–12	13–27	28–40
you are highly unlikely to get an acceptable score under examination conditions and we recommend that you spend a lot of time improving your English before you take IELTS.	you may get an acceptable score under examination conditions but we recommend that you think about having more practice or lessons before you take IELTS.	you are likely to get an acceptable score under examination conditions but remember that different institutions will find different scores acceptable.

ACADEMIC READING

Reading Passage 1, Questions 1–13

1 iii
2 v
3 ii
4 YES
5 YES
6 NO
7 YES
8 NO
9 NOT GIVEN
10 cheese
11 tourism/tourist/tour
12 pottery
13 jewellery/jewelry

Reading Passage 2, Questions 14–26

14 G
15 A
16 H
17 C
18 F
19 I
20 C
21 K
22 E
23 L
24 TRUE
25 NOT GIVEN
26 FALSE

Reading Passage 3, Questions 27–40

27 TRUE
28 TRUE
29 NOT GIVEN
30 FALSE
31 FALSE
32 TRUE
33 FALSE
34 temperatures
35 day-neutral / day-neutral plants
36 food / food resources / adequate food / adequate food resources
37 insects / fertilization by insects
38 rainfall / suitable rainfall
39 sugarcane
40 classification

If you score . . .

0–12	13–28	29–40
you are highly unlikely to get an acceptable score under examination conditions and we recommend that you spend a lot of time improving your English before you take IELTS.	you may get an acceptable score under examination conditions but we recommend that you think about having more practice or lessons before you take IELTS.	you are likely to get an acceptable score under examination conditions but remember that different institutions will find different scores acceptable.

GENERAL TRAINING TEST A

READING

Section 1, Questions 1–14

1	NOT GIVEN
2	NOT GIVEN
3	FALSE
4	NOT GIVEN
5	TRUE
6	FALSE
7	FALSE
8	x
9	i
10	v
11	ii
12	ix
13	iv
14	viii

Section 2, Questions 15–27

15	FALSE
16	NOT GIVEN
17	TRUE
18	FALSE
19	TRUE
20	NOT GIVEN
21	J
22	K
23	E
24	A
25	G
26	I
27	C

Section 3, Questions 28–40

28	A
29	C
30	E
31	F
32	B
33	G
34	E
35	D
36	NOT GIVEN
37	TRUE
38	FALSE
39	FALSE
40	TRUE

If you score . . .

0–16	17–28	29–40
you are highly unlikely to get an acceptable score under examination conditions and we recommend that you spend a lot of time improving your English before you take IELTS.	you may get an acceptable score under examination conditions but we recommend that you think about having more practice or lessons before you take IELTS.	you are likely to get an acceptable score under examination conditions but remember that different institutions will find different scores acceptable.

GENERAL TRAINING TEST B

READING

Section 1, Questions 1–14

1	Weldown
2	10.30 (am)
3	new shoes
4	(the) marshals
5	Fenton
6	every half hour
7	10 kilometre (walk) / 10 kilometer (walk)
8	D
9	F
10	*IN EITHER ORDER; BOTH REQUIRED FOR ONE MARK*
	C (and)
	E
11	G
12	E
13	*IN EITHER ORDER; BOTH REQUIRED FOR ONE MARK*
	D (and)
	G
14	A

Section 2, Questions 15–27

15	TRUE
16	TRUE
17	NOT GIVEN
18	TRUE
19	FALSE
20	FALSE
21	C
22	A
23	D
24	E
25	B
26	D
27	C

Section 3, Questions 28–40

28	D
29	B
30	A
31	B
32	E
33	C
34	NOT GIVEN
35	FALSE
36	NOT GIVEN
37	TRUE
38	FALSE
39	TRUE
40	TRUE

If you score . . .

0–17	18–29	30–40
you are highly unlikely to get an acceptable score under examination conditions and we recommend that you spend a lot of time improving your English before you take IELTS.	you may get an acceptable score under examination conditions but we recommend that you think about having more practice or lessons before you take IELTS.	you are likely to get an acceptable score under examination conditions but remember that different institutions will find different scores acceptable.

Model and sample answers for Writing tasks

TEST 1, WRITING TASK 1

MODEL ANSWER

This model has been prepared by an examiner as an example of a very good answer. However, please note that this is just one example out of many possible approaches.

The graph shows the increase in the ageing population in Japan, Sweden and the USA. It indicates that the percentage of elderly people in all three countries is expected to increase to almost 25% of the respective populations by the year 2040.

In 1940 the proportion of people aged 65 or more stood at only 5% in Japan, approximately 7% in Sweden and 9% in the US. However, while the figures for the Western countries grew to about 15% in around 1990, the figure for Japan dipped to only 2.5% for much of this period, before rising to almost 5% again at the present time.

In spite of some fluctuation in the expected percentages, the proportion of older people will probably continue to increase in the next two decades in the three countries. A more dramatic rise is predicted between 2030 and 2040 in Japan, by which time it is thought that the proportion of elderly people will be similar in the three countries.

TEST 1, WRITING TASK 2

SAMPLE ANSWER

This is an answer written by a candidate who achieved a Band 4 score. Here is the examiner's comment:

It is difficult to find the main arguments in this answer. There are long, formulaic introductions, not many ideas that deal with the actual issues and the writer's point of view is not consistent. The prompt is copied directly three times in the response and the remainder is underlength at 181 words, so marks are lost for this.

The response is organised into sections, but the relationship between ideas is not always clear and the linking expressions are sometimes inaccurate, as in the opening paragraph, or used in a mechanical way, as in the second paragraph.

The dependence on formulaic language and the input material indicates a limited range of vocabulary and there is a lot of repetition and inaccuracy. A range of structures is attempted, but control is weak. Errors in grammar and punctuation are frequent and cause problems for the reader.

According to universities should accept equal numbers of male and female students in every subject. Therefore, this essay will show some reasons of argument for and argument against.

Firstly, I will discuss about two reasons of argument for to begin with universities should accept equal numbers of male and female students in every subject because it will be balance of idea while studying. In general, there usually are different ideas between man and woman. These lead to, new ideas from different vision will happen. Another reason is it display that have equal of society not eccept in each side. In addition, nowadays, the most societies become to accept ability of both in any way.

Secondly, I will discuss about one reason of argument against that is some subjects not suitable for each other. For example, some subject of sports such as weight putting. It is not suitable for female because there are different of body between male and female.

In conclusion, I agree with universities should accept equal numbers of male and female students in every subject. Moreover, it depen on what the subjects that the students want to study, they can choose by themselve because I believe that if the students like to study their subjects, they will do it well so that I strongly agree with this topic.

TEST 2, WRITING TASK 1

SAMPLE ANSWER

This is an answer written by a candidate who achieved a **Band 8** score. Here is the examiner's comment:

> This answer summarises the key features of both charts and integrates them well. Clear trends are identified and supported with appropriately-selected figures. The answer could only be improved by adding an introduction to the general topic of the charts.
>
> The information is well organised, with a clearly-signalled progression. Linking words are used accurately and precisely, although there is occasional omission. Paragraphing is used well initially, but lapses in the later section.
>
> A very good range of vocabulary is used to convey the information concisely and accurately with only occasional inappropriacy. Words are used precisely and there are no errors in spelling or word form.
>
> A wide range of structures is used and most sentences in this answer are accurate. Errors are rare and do not affect communication in this answer.

The first graph shows that there is a gradual decrease in study for career reasons with age. Nearly 80% of students under 26 years, study for their career. This percentage gradually declines by 10-20% every decade. Only 40% of 40-49yr olds and 18% of over 49yr olds are studying for career reasons in late adulthood.

Conversely, the first graph also shows that study stemming from interest increases with age. There are only 10% of under 26yr olds studying out of interest. The percentage increases slowly till the beginning of the fourth decade, and increases dramatically in late adulthood. Nearly same number of 40-49yr olds study for career and interest. However 70% of over 49yr olds study for interest in comparison to 18% studying for career reasons in that age group.

The second graph shows that employer support is maximum (approximately 60%) for the under 26yr students. It drops rapidly to 32% up to the third decade of life, and then increases in late adulthood up to about 44%. It is unclear whether employer support is only for career-focused study, but the highest level is for those students who mainly study for career purposes.

TEST 2, WRITING TASK 2

MODEL ANSWER

This model has been prepared by an examiner as an example of a very good answer. However, please note that this is just one example out of many possible approaches.

It is quite common these days for young people in many countries to have a break from studying after graduating from high school. The trend is not restricted to rich students who have the money to travel, but is also evident among poorer students who choose to work and become economically independent for a period of time.

The reasons for this trend may involve the recognition that a young adult who passes directly from school to university is rather restricted in terms of general knowledge and experience of the world. By contrast, those who have spent some time earning a living or travelling to other places, have a broader view of life and better personal resources to draw on. They tend to be more independent, which is a very important factor in academic study and research, as well as giving them an advantage in terms of coping with the challenges of student life.

However, there are certainly dangers in taking time off at that important age. Young adults may end up never returning to their studies or finding it difficult to readapt to an academic environment. They may think that it is better to continue in a particular job, or to do something completely different from a university course. But overall, I think this is less likely today, when academic qualifications are essential for getting a reasonable career.

My view is that young people should be encouraged to broaden their horizons. That is the best way for them to get a clear perspective of what they are hoping to do with their lives and why. Students with such a perspective are usually the most effective and motivated ones and taking a year off may be the best way to gain this.

TEST 3, WRITING TASK 1

MODEL ANSWER

This model has been prepared by an examiner as an example of a very good answer. However, please note that this is just one example out of many possible approaches.

The map shows two proposed locations for a new supermarket for the town of Garlsdon.

The first potential location (S1) is outside the town itself, and is sited just off the main road to the town of Hindon, lying 12 kms to the north-west. This site is in the countryside and so would be able to accommodate a lot of car parking. This would make it accessible to shoppers from both Hindon and Garlsdon who could travel by car. As it is also close to the railway line linking the two towns to Cransdon (25 km to the south-east), a potentially large number of shoppers would also be able to travel by train.

In contrast, the suggested location, S2, is right in the town centre, which would be good for local residents. Theoretically the store could be accessed by road or rail from the surrounding towns, including Bransdon, but as the central area is a no-traffic zone, cars would be unable to park and access would be difficult.

Overall, neither site is appropriate for all the towns, but for customers in Cransdon, Hindon and Garlsdon, the out-of-town site (S1) would probably offer more advantages.

TEST 3, WRITING TASK 2

SAMPLE ANSWER

This is an answer written by a candidate who achieved a **Band 6** score. Here is the examiner's comment:

Although the answer considers the main issues in the question, it deals much more with the aspect of 'competition' than it does with 'co-operation'. Some of the supporting examples are overdeveloped and divert the reader away from the argument. However, the main points are relevant and the writer's point of view is generally clear.

The argument has a logical progression and there is some good use of linking expressions, though the use of rhetorical questions to signal topic changes is not very skilful. There are also examples of overusing markers, and of errors in referencing.

The candidate tries to use a range of language, but there are regular errors in word choice and word form, and this occasionally causes problems for the reader. Similarly, a range of structures is attempted, but not always with good control of punctuation or grammar. However, the meaning is generally clear.

Nowadays, purpose of education being changed in Korea. There are some people who think that competition in children should be made, also others believe that children who are taught to co-operate as well as become more useful adults. There are advantages and disadvantages for both of the arguements.

To begin with, what is good if a sense of competition in children is made? They could develope themselves more and more as they learn and study a lot to win from the competition. To prove this, in Korea, it is popular – even common now – to have a tutor who come to student's house to teach extra pieces of study with paying a lot of money. They learn faster than what they learn at school. Furthermore, during the vacations, students study abroad to learn English for a month instead of revise school work. If they have experiments such as study abroad, it is one of the greatest plus point to go to the famous well-known high-school. Moreover, there are four big school exam and two national examinations to test students' level of studies. Generally, only the highest 40% can go to the good quality highschools and colleges. children learn as much as they can, to win the competition to obtain good quality schools.

On the other hand, as they are busy to enter the schools and study individually with their own tutors, there are problems. They become selfish. They become careless and don't help others alot if it is about studies. There will be no co-operations for them. Then, why are there companies for many people to work in? Each of them are clever, however, there are weak parts and strong parts for each person. To co-operate is to improve this part. People talk and listen to what others thinking of and learn. That could also be a great opportunity to learn instead of learning alone with one teacher.

In conclusion, I strongly agree with that children should be taught to co-operate rather than compete. Nobody is perfect. People learn together, work together to develop each other. Therefore, I want parents and teachers to educate children concentrating on co-operation, not compete and ranking them.

TEST 4, WRITING TASK 1

SAMPLE ANSWER

This is an answer written by a candidate who achieved a **Band 7** score. Here is the examiner's comment:

This answer selects and describes the information well. Key features are clearly identified, while unexpected differences are highlighted and illustrated. The answer is relevant and accurate with a clear overview.

Information is well-organised using a good range of signals and link words. These are generally accurate and appropriate, although occasional errors occur.

The writer successfully uses some less common words. There is a clear awareness of style but there are occasional inaccuracies and there is some repetition. Grammar is well-controlled and sentences are varied and generally accurate with only minor errors.

The table shows the details regarding the underground railway systems in six cities.

London has the oldest underground railway systems among the six cities. It was opened in the year 1863, and it is already 140 years old. Paris is the second oldest, in which it was opened in the year 1900. This was then followed by the opening of the railway systems in Tokyo, Washington DC and Kyoto. Los Angeles has the newest underground railway system, and was only opened in the year 2001. In terms of the size of the railway systems, London, for certain, has the largest underground railway systems. It has 394 kilometres of route in total, which is nearly twice as large as the system in Paris. Kyoto, in contrast, has the smallest system. It only has 11 kilometres of route, which is more than 30 times less than that of London.

Interestingly, Tokyo, which only has 155 kilometres of route, serves the greatest number of passengers per year, at 1927 millions passengers. The system in Paris has the second greatest number of passengers, at 1191 millions passengers per year. The smalest underground railway system, Kyoto, serves the smallest number of passengers per year as predicted.

In conclusion, the underground railway systems in different cities vary a lot in the size of the system, the number of passengers served per year and in the age of the system.

TEST 4, WRITING TASK 2

MODEL ANSWER

This model has been prepared by an examiner as an example of a very good answer. However, please note that this is just one example out of many possible approaches.

Today the way we consider human psychology and mental development is heavily influenced by the genetic sciences. We now understand the importance of inherited characteristics more than ever before. Yet we are still unable to decide whether an individual's personality and development are more influenced by genetic factors (nature) or by the environment (nurture).

Research, relating to identical twins, has highlighted how significant inherited characteristics can be for an individual's life. But whether these characteristics are able to develop within the personality of an individual surely depends on whether the circumstances allow such a development. It seems that the experiences we have in life are so unpredictable and so powerful, that they can boost or over-ride other influences, and there seems to be plenty of research findings to confirm this.

My own view is that there is no one major influence in a person's life. Instead, the traits we inherit from our parents and the situations and experiences that we encounter in life are constantly interacting. It is the interaction of the two that shapes a person's personality and dictates how that personality develops. If this were not true, then we would be able to predict the behaviour and character of a person from the moment they were born.

In conclusion, I do not think that either nature or nurture is the major influence on a person, but that both have powerful effects. How these factors interact is still unknown today and they remain largely unpredictable in a person's life.

TEST A, WRITING TASK 1 (GENERAL TRAINING)

MODEL ANSWER

This model has been prepared by an examiner as an example of a very good answer. However, please note that this is just one example out of many possible approaches.

Dear James,

I was very shocked to get your letter saying that the noise from my flat has been spoiling your evenings and causing you some distress. I am really, really sorry about that. I had no idea that you would be able to hear so much, so I hope you will accept my apologies.

As you may have guessed, I am trying to refit my kitchen in the evenings when I get home from work. Unfortunately it is all taking longer than expected and I have been having problems with getting things to fit properly. This has meant a lot of banging and hammering.

As the kitchen is still not finished, I have decided to call in a professional builder who will finish the work in the next day or two. He'll work only during daytime hours, so you won't be disturbed in the evenings again, I promise.

Sorry to have caused these problems,

Bill.

TEST A, WRITING TASK 2 (GENERAL TRAINING)

SAMPLE ANSWER

This is an answer written by a candidate who achieved a **Band 7** score. Here is the examiner's comment:

> The answer addresses both ideas put forward in the task, and the writer's point of view is clearly stated throughout. He presents relevant main ideas and draws appropriate conclusions from these. However, the response is unfinished and this means that some of the ideas are rather generalised and would need more support. The opening sentence is copied and the whole answer is underlength, so it loses marks for this.
>
> The writing has clear organisation and some sophisticated use of link words and referencing. However, paragraphing is not always logical as it is organised by sentences rather than topics.
>
> The range of vocabulary and structures is very good with a high level of control and precision. Complex ideas are expressed in a sophisticated way and most sentences are accurate. There are only rare errors, e.g. in spelling and subject/verb agreement.

To a large extent, I believe that children are given too much free time.

Free time in my opinion refers to time not spent under the direct supervision of a parent, teacher or a person enthrusted with the responsibility of bringing up the child.

Such time is often spent on several things such as watching television, playing with friends, going to parties, doing home work, playing games on their own amongst others.

Amongst all of the above, a child could either be influenced by his or her peer group especially when left without attention or be influenced by what he or she watches on television most of which are those not meant to be viewed by the child's age group.

In my opinion, most of the formative years of a child should be spent doing school work, engaging in recreational activities that would develop the child emotionally and mentally. I believe this strongly because at a young age, a child is quick to grasp most of all that is seen or heard.

For instance, a child who is not used to doing more school work (usually referred to as house work

TEST B, WRITING TASK 1 (GENERAL TRAINING)

SAMPLE ANSWER

This is an answer written by a candidate who achieved a **Band 5** score. Here is the examiner's comment:

> The reason for writing is very clear in this letter but it is not clear who the letter is to. The writer gives information to cover all three bullet points, but only one is well extended, and the whole response is underlength at 135 words, so it loses marks for this.
>
> The information is organised and it is easy to follow the message. A range of linkers is used across the answer and they are generally accurate, but in some places, especially the first paragraph, sentences are not well-linked.
>
> The range of vocabulary is sufficient for the task and there are some quite precise expressions. There are no errors in word form, but some very basic spelling errors occur. In terms of grammar, the range is rather limited with many very short sentences and few complex structures. Grammar is generally well-controlled, however, with only a few minor errors and occasional inappropriate punctuation.

Dear Sir or Madam,

My name is Mohamad Abdul. Iam taking apart-time evening course. I am having a hard time keeping up with this course. I am affraid I cannot continue the course.

My problem is, I have a full-time job, from 9am – 5pm. Sometimes, I am asked to stay extra hours, to finish up the rest of the work. That is because the holidays are coming up soon. Also, I have to do some work preperations for the next day.

At night when I get home, I am too tired to even prepare adinner for myself. Also, I have no time to study for this course.

I would like dropp this course this quarter. Then take it again the next quarter. so, please accept my situation.

Thank you for your cooperation
sincerely
M. Abdul

TEST B, WRITING TASK 2 (GENERAL TRAINING)

MODEL ANSWER

This model has been prepared by an examiner as an example of a very good answer. However, please note that this is just one example out of many possible approaches.

I think it is true that in almost every country today each household and family produces a large amount of waste every week. Most of this rubbish comes from the packaging from the things we buy, such as processed food. But even if we buy fresh food without packaging, we still produce rubbish from the plastic bags used everywhere to carry shopping home.

The reason why we have so much packaging is that we consume so much more on a daily basis than families did in the past. Convenience is also very important in modern life, so we buy packaged or canned food that can be transported from long distances and stored until we need it, first in the supermarket, and then at home.

However, I think the amount of waste produced is also a result of our tendency to use something once and throw it away. We forget that even the cheapest plastic bag has used up valuable resources and energy to produce. We also forget that it is a source of pollution and difficult to dispose of.

I think, therefore, that governments need to raise this awareness in the general public. Children can be educated about environmental issues at school, but adults need to take action. Governments can encourage such action by putting taxes on packaging, such as plastic bags, by providing recycling services and by fining households and shops that do not attempt to recycle their waste.

With the political will, such measures could really reduce the amount of rubbish we produce. Certainly nobody wants to see our resources used up and our planet poisoned by waste.

Sample answer sheets

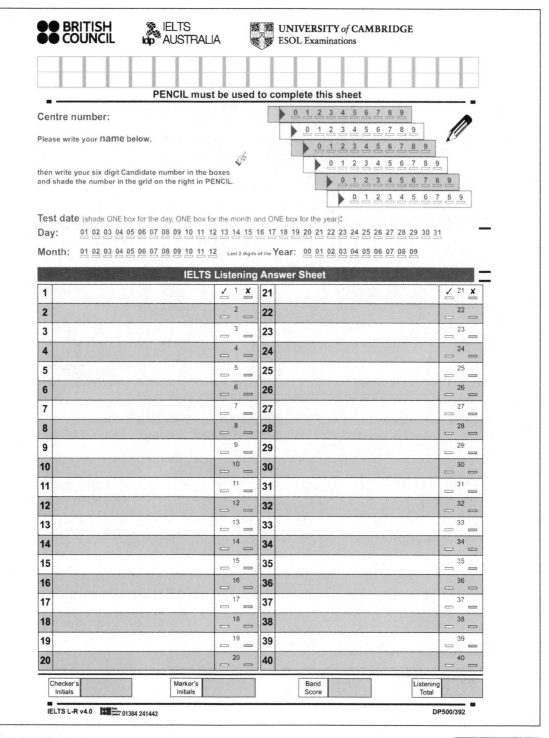

Are you: Female? ▭   Male? ▭

Your first language code: ▶ 0 1 2 3 4 5 6 7 8 9
▶ 0 1 2 3 4 5 6 7 8 9
▶ 0 1 2 3 4 5 6 7 8 9

IELTS Reading Answer Sheet

Module taken (shade one box):   Academic ▭   General Training ▭

		✓ 1 ✗			✓ 21 ✗
1			21		
2		2	22		22
3		3	23		23
4		4	24		24
5		5	25		25
6		6	26		26
7		7	27		27
8		8	28		28
9		9	29		29
10		10	30		30
11		11	31		31
12		12	32		32
13		13	33		33
14		14	34		34
15		15	35		35
16		16	36		36
17		17	37		37
18		18	38		38
19		19	39		39
20		20	40		40

Checker's Initials		Marker's Initials		Band Score		Reading Total	

Acknowledgements

The authors and publishers are grateful to the following for permission to use copyright material. While every effort has been made, it has not been possible to identify the sources to all of the material used and in such cases the publishers would welcome information from the copyright owners. Apologies are expressed for any omissions.

The publishers are grateful to the following for permission to reproduce copyright material:

For the adapted extract on pp. 16–17: 'Dr Johnson's Dictionary' from *The Story of English* by Robert McCrum, William Cran, and Robert MacNeil. © 1986. Reproduced by permission of Faber and Faber; for the extract on pp. 20–21: 'Nature or Nuture' from *Paradigms Lost* by John L Casti. Copyright © 1989 John L Casti. Used by permission of The Warner Book Group and John L Casti; for the extract on pp. 24–25: 'The Truth about the Environment' by Bjorn Lomborg in *The Economist* 4 August 2001, and for the extract on pp. 71–72: 'AI by another name' in *The Economist Technology Quarterly* 16 March 2002. © The Economist Newspaper Limited, London; for the extract on pp. 38–39: 'Bakelite, The Birth of modern plastics' from *Bakelite Style* by Tessa Clark. © 1997 Quintet Publishing Ltd; for the extract on pp. 43–44: 'Comic Relief' by John McCrone, published in *New Scientist* 27 May 2000 and for the extract on pp. 89–90: 'Flawed Beauty', by David Cohen, published in *New Scientist* 22 September 2001. © New Scientist Ltd; for the extract on pp. 48–49: 'The Development of Scientific English' from *English: History, Diversity and Change* by David Graddol. © 1996 Routledge. Reproduced by permission of Taylor & Francis Books UK; for the extract on pp. 62–63: 'Early Childhood Education' published in *Is Something Missing from Early Childhood Education?* Written by Dr Lockwood Smith. Used by kind permission of Dr Lockwood Smith; for the extract on pp. 67–68: 'Disappearing Delta' by Laura Penvenne, published in *American Scientist, Volume 84*. Used by kind permission of Laura Penvenne; for the adapted text on pp. 86–87 'A Fragile Balance' taken from *The Geographical Journal*, September 1994. Used by permission of Blackwell Publishing; for the adapted extract on pp. 109–110 'Lack of Sleep' from *The Weekend Telegraph*, November 1997. © The Telegraph Group Limited; for the adapted extract on pp. 123–124: *Glow-worms*. Written by John Tyler. © 1994. Used by kind permission of John Tyler.

Design concept by Peter Ducker MSTD

Cover design by John Dunne

The cassettes and audio CDs which accompany this book were recorded at Studio AVP, London.